AMERICANS
AND
NOTHING
ELSE

AMERICANS
AND
NOTHING
ELSE

TREVOR FISHLOCK

CASSELL
LONDON

CASSELL LTD.
35 Red Lion Square, London WC1R 4SG
and at Sydney, Auckland, Toronto, Johannesburg,
an affiliate of
Macmillan Publishing Co., Inc.,
New York.

First published 1980

ISBN 0 304 30638 X

Printed in Great Britain by
Richard Clay (The Chaucer Press) Ltd.
Bungay, Suffolk

FOR PENNY

CONTENTS

Seattle
WASHINGTON
MONTANA
NORTH DAKOT
OREGON
SOUTH DAKOT
IDAHO
Yellowstone
Deadwood
Pierre
Jackson
Hole
Rapid
City
Idaho Falls
WYOMING
Badlands
NEBRAS
Salt Lake
City
NEVADA
Denver
San Francisco
UTAH
COLORADO
CALIFORNIA
KANS
Las Vegas
Grand Canyon
Flagstaff
OK
Los Angeles
ARIZONA
NEW MEXICO
Phoenix
TEXA
Austi
San An
Towns & cities visited   o
Road travel
Rail travel

MINNESOTA
Grand Marais
Duluth
WISCONSIN
Minneapolis
St Paul
Pipestone
Worthington
IOWA
MICHIGAN
Detroit
Chicago
Grinnell
Des Moines
Omaha
ILLINOIS
INDIANA
OHIO
MAINE
Bangor
VT.
N.H.
NEW YORK
MASS.
Boston
Hartford
R.I.
CONN.
New York
N.J.
PENNSYLVANIA
Pittsburgh
Baltimore
Washington
DEL.
MD.
WEST VIRGINIA
Richmond
VIRGINIA
St Louis
MISSOURI
KENTUCKY
NORTH CAROLINA
Nashville
Oak Ridge
Fayetteville
TENNESSEE
Memphis
ARKANSAS
Chattanooga
SOUTH CAROLINA
Little Rock
Atlanta
Birmingham
MISS.
ALABAMA
GEORGIA
Savannah
Vicksburg
LOUISIANA
FLORIDA
Baton Rouge
Cape Canaveral
Houston
New Orleans
Orlando
St Petersburg
0   Miles   500

PREFACE

It was my good fortune to be awarded a travelling fellowship in the United States of America. I have to admit that I had the time of my life. This is not to say that I liked everything I saw and did. There were times when roads seemed endless, and times of tedium and fatigue. But enjoyment outweighed all else. I believe, I certainly hope, that I approached this opportunity to explore the country and listen to its people, open-eyed, and open-minded, with judicious balancing dashes of naîvety and scepticism. I travelled sometimes in company, sometimes alone; and although there was a programme of travel, I was also able on many occasions to undertake my own expeditions and pursue my own interests.

I started in the middle, in the mid-West, and worked outwards, so that I arrived in places like New York fairly well into the experience; and I think this was a good way of doing it. Along the way I encountered much kindness, good humour, friendly interest and generosity. A list of everyone who helped me would be very long; but some representative names include David and Karen Lanegran, Don and Susan Dwight, Jim and Florence Vance, Ted Miller, Paul and Pat Sherburne and Jim Brandenburg, who all live in Minnesota.

As I say, there were many others, in many parts of the United States, and they all helped to reveal something of America to me. My deep thanks to them all. My thanks, too, to

Simon Scott of Cassell, whose enthusiasm and encouragement were a necessary spur, and to Mary Griffith, who went through the manuscript with her usual understanding, good humour and meticulous care. Meanwhile, typing it, encouraging, brow-mopping, there was my wife Penny, indispensable, whose name means patience.

T.F.
London, 1979

1
AMERICAN PIE

The United States themselves are essentially the greatest poem.

Walt Whitman

As ice clunked gently like alpine cowbells in the thick bourbon tumblers of the sacred cocktail hour, there was always someone there with an earnest smooth face and trousers too short: a businessman. American businessmen tend to wear trousers that fail to be long enough and they show as much ankle as Victorian coquettes. Their cutty pants make their suits look curiously ill-fitting as if the wearers are schoolboys who have been persuaded by their mothers to carry on with their old suits a few weeks longer, on the understanding that they will be bought new ones next term.

They are a race of serious men, and I supposed that any latent sense of humour had been excised at business school. They would swim up alongside and peer at my buttonhole identity badge.

'Is that right your hospitals are falling down because of socialized medicine?'

'Jesus, your taxes. You poor suckers.'

'Everybody on welfare. The government interfering in everything. Can you beat that?'

'Those strikes of yours. Doesn't anybody want to make money?'

'The British disease, huh?'

'You pay that for gas? How can you live in a country like that?'

When I got back home, a friend of mine, a xenophobe to his marrow, said: 'Don't tell me — you hated it. America: what a country. Lucky you weren't mugged or shot. Or worse. Shooting each other is what Americans do in their spare time. Kids get guns in their Christmas crackers.'

'Well, it's true that it's an armed society and there's a lot of violence,' I said. 'But I felt safe enough in city streets; and I stayed in places where people feel so secure they don't lock their doors and they feel no need to lock up their cars. Once, in St Louis, I left my wallet full of money in a hotel room and the chambermaid posted it on to me intact. Another time I left my pocket-book in a phone box in Iowa, and someone sent it all the way home to Britain.'

He pressed on. 'I remember Americans from the war. All nylons for the girls and chocolate for the kids. And big talk. And why do they shout all the time? I bet you lived on chewing gum and hamburgers while you were over there. I've heard their food's terrible. They pour syrup on their sausages and bacon and eat ice cream in the middle of the night. It's uncivilized. Revolting.'

'It's all a matter of taste and custom,' I said. 'Take the Japanese: they eat badgers and baby bumblebees but they think roast lamb is disgusting and take their suits to the cleaners if they've been anywhere near it. And the Americans think our butchers' shops are strange. They have a fetish about hygiene and they wonder why we don't all get hepatitis with the meat displayed in the open like that.'

He reflected a moment.

'Their beer's awful isn't it?'

'Fairly awful,' I conceded. 'But they think our beer is too warm.'

He made a *moue* of contempt. 'People I know who've been over there say the beer is gnat pee and they've got more money than they know what to do with and they ruin everything with ice.'

Thus was closed the subject of the United States of America.

On the other side of the Atlantic there was much the same sort of thing. 'I was in a British hotel once. You know: no bathroom. And when I asked for some ice, Jesus, I thought they were going to make a federal case out of it.'

2

In Minnesota once, for reasons arcane, the audience at a theatre rose to their feet to sing Land of Hope and Glory. As I rose too, I felt this to be a slightly mad experience.

'Say, why aren't you singing, you're English aren't you?' my neighbour hissed from behind her programme, noticing my still lips.

'Because the words are absurd,' I muttered back, as the audience flung themselves at it for all the world like the mob at the last night of the proms.

'What's the matter, aren't you proud of your country?' she re-hissed, scandalized, lasering me with her bright eyes.

'I'm not sure,' I whispered.

'*Wider still and wider*!' she sang at me, hoping I would feel ashamed. 'Sing up!'

'I don't know the words,' I said.

'My God,' she said. 'Well, I'm proud of my country.'

'But it's not even your song.'

'*Make thee mightier yet*!' she sang defiantly, eyes staring shinily at some unseen flag.

Afterwards I tried to explain that even Elgar had not liked the way his big tune had been turned into jingo slosh. But I could see there was a gulf between us and she felt puzzled. After all, Americans put their hands on their hearts and swear allegiance to the stars and stripes. And I felt a shade guilty about my lack of fervour because she and some friends had just bought me a large dinner. The main course had been a Humphrey Bogart, a slab of spare ribs of beef as large as a typewriter; and this had been followed by a hot fudge sundae, described in the novella of a menu as a canopy of whipped cream and nuts over thick creamy hot fudge, made with vanilla ice cream, topped with crushed nuts. The menu, I noted, had this rather sickly birthday card verse:

> Wives who cook and do the dishes
> Should be granted these three wishes:
> A grateful mate, a well-kissed cheek,
> A restaurant dinner every week!

For that the least I could have done was sing.

The whole episode that evening had been a little shorthand scribble of some of the facets of America: manifest abundance, generosity and unselfconscious patriotism. Even though it was somebody else's anthem.

I always had an itch, that sometimes became an ache, to see America; so that when I knew I was going to spend the best part of a year there the excitement was coupled with a relief that I was going to be able to rub the itch. The writer H.L. Mencken called his country the greatest show on earth, and I was sure I would find out that he was right. Mary Antin, who emigrated from Russia in 1894 when she was thirteen, recalled in her book *The Promised Land*: 'So at last I was going to America! The boundaries burst. The arch of heaven soared. A million suns shone out for every star. The winds rushed in from outer space...'

My goodness.

I did not feel like that exactly. But the sense of anticipation was all-consuming. There was the sniff of an adventure in the offing.

America first seeped into my consciousness and imagination when I was five years old, through the films at my local Regal which featured Gene Autry, Roy Rogers, Gabby Hayes, Hopalong Cassidy, the Three Stooges and the Bowery Boys. Later there were Bogart and Cagney. I learned about America's landscape, cities, cars, social life and the qualities of its fighting men from films at a time when we attended the cinema on fixed days of the week and watched whatever was showing, rather than selecting films to see.

I remember being scolded for chewing gum — 'filthy American habit'. We were told by teachers that the smudgy and garish American comics we read in the school playground were trash and a bad influence. We were steered away from Superman to the worthier pastures of the *Children's Newspaper*. Somehow, in the years when my height was increasing from four feet to five, there was implanted in my mind the idea that things American were risqué or undesirable; that well-brought-up children avoided them. 'Say yes,' we were told. 'Only Americans say yeah.' Thus America seemed forbidden and irresistible.

I noted from the films I watched that Americans had curious table manners, eating with a fork only, and generally eating rapidly, as if food were an inconvenience. They ate often in chemists' shops, which they called drugstores. In a scene which stuck in my memory a young man confronted with a breakfast cooked by his doting Mom simply emptied the plate on to a slice of bread, jammed another on top, and hurried off with his mouth stuffed with this makeshift sandwich. I admired that sort of panache. In another film a man slouched into a small restaurant and asked for blueberry pie. After that I longed for blueberry pie and waited twenty years for it. It was the first thing I ate in America, but I made the mistake of buying it in a fast-food restaurant, and it was too sweet, and disappointing.

Almost the first long books I read were *Tom Sawyer* and *Huckleberry Finn*, which entranced me and which I re-read often. I also read James Fenimore Cooper. But neither at primary school nor secondary school did I learn anything of the United States: it was not on the menu. The War of Independence was dealt with briefly, but that was all. I suppose it was considered that American history ended in 1776.

To me, as a boy, it seemed that Americans lived either among skyscrapers or on the range, either in tenements or ranch houses. They seemed more God-fearing than us, but also more rumbustious, freewheeling, relaxed and violent, and they droved around in monstrous, lumbering wagons of cars. They had short jabs of names, like Chuck, Brad and Hank.

Apart from seeing America in films I began to read about it in the newspapers and particularly in the popular papers which supplied a daily column of snippets of the bizarre. Thus, on top of my earlier impressions were laid images of war, McCarthy, multiple divorces, people squatting atop flagpoles, hold-ups, Doris Day and the electric chair. Fifties television showed me a people who screamed with laughter for a long time at mild or unfunny jokes, and who, infuriatingly, applauded a singer after he had sung the first three words of a song.

The first Americans I met as a boy were the crews of warships which used to visit Portsmouth, the ships being opened to the public. The Americans seemed to me taller and paler than Britons, with hair strangely short, like fur, and uniforms more gaudily decorated. Their chevrons were upside down and they had difficult foreign names on their chest tags.

They talked loudly, and they seemed much more at ease and

less formal than their British counterparts; and the ratings had unsmart sloppy soft hats which adults, who had served in His Majesty's Forces, sniffily considered to be evidence of lower standards in the US fleet. The fact that there was no rum, the drink of tars, or, indeed, any other liquor on American warships, was considered evidence by adults of the superiority of the British matelot vis-à-vis the Yanks. Over the ships' loud-speakers a voice would intone: 'Now hear this, now hear this,' and this to me was evidence of the veracity of American films. Later I observed American tourists from time to time. The men had brighter clothing than we in Britain were used to, and loud check trousers which contrasted with the British street uniform of grey suit, white shirt and maroon tie. Almost all American men were called Elmer, Henree or Dear, and the women had fancy hair; and I noted that they all talked loudly and excited-ly, so that to my earlier notions of America was added the idea that its people were exuberant, noisily curious and not capable of quiet conversation.

So it was that I ended my teenage, like the majority of British people, knowing about America only slightly more than damn-all. I was an adult before I met a real American to talk to and before I read a history of America or serious American novels.

Because of the nature of popular journalism, film drama and our education, our received picture of America and Americans is a lop-sided one. If it is any consolation their view of us is equally unbalanced and uninformed. Many Americans do not know that Britain is so small, that, being only as large as New York State and Pennsylvania put together, it could be tucked under America's arm. Their ideas about us and other parts of the world are often hazy. A recent government survey showed, for example, that twenty-seven per cent of American high school students thought that Golda Meir was president of Egypt.

Through films and television we know the streets of New York well, just as Americans know the sights of London. But New York is not America, nor London Britain. Exploration of the wider America, the ordinary and extraordinary, remains a revealing and satisfying and surprising adventure. At least I found it so. It is also chastening and saddening sometimes, and irritating and perplexing.

No less than it was years ago, the prospect of America remains intriguing and exciting, a hyperventilation of the imagination. How can it be otherwise? The American experience and adventure is still, as it has been for three centuries, enthralling — as ambiguous and as enigmatic as it is worrying as it is intoxicating.

For Europeans the fascination is singular. Americans are the people we might have been. As it happened, our grandfathers and great-grandfathers stayed at home. But their brothers and cousins and neighbours made the move, so that when we see their descendants we see ourselves uncannily transported to another existence; our cousins at the Atlantic remove are much the same in some respects, of course, but manifestly different in others. The mirror we look into is deliciously and disturbingly distorted.

2

Late one night, eyes gritty and mouth gluey from a long flight, I found myself in the middle of America, in a room full of foreigners and assorted Americans. Someone put a can of thin cold beer into my hand, and the foreigners began to inspect me, and I them. There was an Argentinian, a Brazilian, an Ecuadorian, a Hong Kong Chinese, an Israeli, a Cameroonian, a Tanzanian, a Japanese, a Thai and a Swede. We were soon to learn that our melting-pot would be the magic ingredient of our joint inspection of America; and that, whether we liked it or not, we were going to be as close as the plies in plywood for eight months.

I was dunked into that melting-pot quite by lucky chance. While turning idly through a magazine one day I saw an advertisement offering a British journalist a travelling fellowship in the United States. It was open to competition and, as good fortune had it, I eventually won it. I gave up salary, took leave of absence and went off, as Simon and Garfunkel had it, 'to look for America.' The fellowship was offered by the World Press Institute which is attached to Macalester College, a middle-class arts college with sixteen hundred students, at St Paul in Minnesota. The institute was founded in 1962 and provides a programme of study and travel for groups of foreign journalists. It is funded by a variety of companies and corporations. Its travelling fellowship offers as comprehensive a study of Americans in their natural habitat as is possible in that time.

That year, the eleven of us, a woman and ten men, were newspaper journalists and broadcasters mainly in our early thirties. Six were from countries where the freedom of the press is circumscribed. We made a singular flying circus. We went by air, by bus, by car, by canoe, by mule, from the Canadian border to the edge of Mexico, from New York to San Francisco, from Seattle to Florida; ranging 'the varied and ample land,' as Walt Whitman wrote; from log cabin to White House, from dense pine forest to desert, from mountain peak to canyon floor; from teeming rushing cities to tranquil slow hamlets; 'from sea to shining sea,'; through thirty-eight of the fifty states.

We visited large industries and small businesses, banks, farms, docks, mills; Indian reservations and ghettos; penthouses and opulent homes of rich men; prisons and army camps and boardrooms; schools and hospitals; newpapers and magazines and television studios. We met politicians, policemen, sheriffs, generals, surgeons, astronauts, criminals, lobbyists, social workers, teachers, prisoners, jailers, defence strategists, ranchers, architects, doctors, Mexicans, Indian chiefs, black leaders, Chinese leaders, union leaders, sportsmen, editors, car workers, atom bomb makers, soldiers, down and outs, students, children, lawyers, diplomats, professors, and even a leader of militant prostitutes (my mind boggled, too).

We saw America red in tooth and claw, warts and all, good and bad. Nothing was ever hidden, to my knowledge, no embarrassment kept secret.

Before I went to America I was asked by the fellowship staff how I thought I would 'relate in the group dynamics situation.' Many Americans are absorbed by the study of themselves and how they 'relate' to each other, to their spouses and to society. They like to observe and explain themselves and they like to use jargon as the medium of self-analysis. Of course, I had no idea what relating in the group dynamics situation meant; although once I had learned to speak American I found that it meant:

'How do you get on with people?' The meaning of the question became apparent fairly shortly after our black, white, brown and yellow team began its dizzying progress. What happens when you pluck eleven people of disparate race and background, of differing outlook, personality, temperament, values and dietary habits — and send them on an exacting and remarkable tour of the endlessly amazing and complex United States, quartering them closely together for eight months so that they share rooms, buses, cars, meals, parties, swimming pools, saunas, interviews, tents and even clothing?

Well, there were no homicides.

We had some advice, like: 'Be tolerant. Relate to one another.'

And, more practically: 'Shower often.'

The roads were long and people sometimes felt homesick and there were occasional frustrations and tiredness. Some coped better than others. But I felt at the time, and still do, that being part of a multi-national group was a stimulating and rewarding part of the journey, not least because it enabled us to look at America, not through our eyes only, but also through the eyes of ten others with different perspectives. It was a constant and instructive process, even if there was an occasional gritting of the teeth at hearing a dear colleague ask the same question for the one hundredth time.

Out of it all, though, we forged companionship. For myself I struck up some firm friendships which not only survived the enforced and prolonged intimacy of our travelling, but were indeed strengthened by it. Our competence in English varied widely, sometimes wildly, and we developed a group patois and a private humour. The sardonic outlook and wit of the Israeli was mixed with the jollity of a Chinese, the wryness of an Argentinian, the belly-laugh of a Tanzanian, the survival humour of a Swede, the glee of a Thai, the straight-faced jokes of a Japanese and the indescribable humour of an Englishman, all flowing through the medium of a fractured English. The product was a rare brew.

3

It is not difficult, even today, to comprehend the excitement and awe of people who migrated from Europe, gulped the new air and began to feel that the pie was there for the cutting; that anything seemed possible. It is partly a matter of the immensity of America. It is hard to describe, but the very vastness of the land provides a certain sense of release, a filling of lungs and mind. In Britain no place is more than eighty miles from the sea. In the mid-West of America I met a lot of people who had never seen the ocean. It may be a cliché to remark on America's size, but it would be a poor reporter who did not. The vastness is an element of the excitement and it is especially impressive to Europeans whose vistas have been confined.

Also, it is not only a matter of vastness, of geographical room. There is also more room for imagination, for the satisfying of appetite and whim because Americans have determinedly thrown off Old World shackles. In America, in many ways, the reins are looser. It is not true to say that anything goes; but a lot more goes than it does almost anywhere else. The social and economic restraints that apply in other parts of the world have been thrown off or modified in America. The boundaries in living styles have been rolled back. Americans ask, not why, but why not?

Because very little in America is understated the quality of chiaroscuro is sharp and startling. American life has a quality of bustle, of primary colours and constant appeals and assaults to the senses that is bewildering to a newcomer. For some of the other foreigners I travelled with the effect of America was profound and disturbing. They had come from societies where traditions and social mores, and systems of government, were usually stricter, and certainly very different. The spectacle of sprawling, bubbling, freewheeling, loose-belted America, big and noisy, and evidently enjoying the unbounded way of life, came to them first as a shock. After some wary sips, however, even the most buttoned-up began to relax and to take deeper draughts. But the dazzling side of America also accentuated the sense of shock at what they observed of the dark side, the devastation of the Bronx and other slums, the condition of the black Americans, the unhappiness of Indians, the evidence of callousness and indifference in the American character to those at the bottom of the heap, the failures of the American system, and the thick, ugly, hopeless stratum of violence.

The imperfections they saw in the system struck them in various ways. For some there was disappointment. If America, land of abundance and freedom, could not provide for all its people a simple justice, what hope was there for less fortunate societies? For some there was confirmation that the aggressive, open American way, with its emphasis on success, had failed because the record sheet was so stained with the sweat of slaves, the blood of red men, the odour of slums, the whiff of cordite and the stink of Vietnam. I saw at times a fleeting smile of *Schadenfreude*.

The contrasts in our odyssey were astonishing, even for minds which quite quickly became elastic. We would lunch on unsavoury hamburgers in a smelly café in the smashed-up terrifying hopeless slum of the Bronx, watched by suspicious and resentful eyes; and dine with rich men in Manhattan's towers, all in one day.

It takes time to adjust to America's contrasts and its paradoxes and contradictions. And there are many of them. Poverty sits thigh by thigh with abundance. In places of plenty and beauty people go in fear of sudden violence. Black people have still a long road to tread: 'Life, Liberty and the Pursuit of Happiness,' as the Declaration of Independence had it, are still harder for blacks than for whites. It is a country with millions of decent, hard-working, church-going, generous, peaceable people, armed to the teeth. On the whole they detest militarism because they are resentful of authority in any form; but they like soldiers and they love flags. And in the land which is the polar opposite of a totalitarian state, where communism has as much chance of rooting as an orchid on an iceberg, they can still exhibit a pathological fear of communism which, to an outsider, looks in its intensity as bizarre as it is unreasonable.

4

The first three months of the fellowship were anchored to the college; and, although there were expeditions to Detroit and Chicago, to Dakota, Deadwood and Denver, much of our time in this period was spent in Minnesota, in Minneapolis and St Paul, which are nicknamed the Twin Cities. They are divided by the Mississippi River and united by the belief that the inhabitants on the other side of the river are inferior. Being on the eastern bank, St Paul was settled first, and it is the capital of Minnesota. It is smaller than Minneapolis, and staider; somewhat grandfatherly in its pace, compared with sparkier Minneapolis. St Paul was settled mainly by Irish and German Catholics, and Minneapolis by Scandinavians and westering Yankees. St Paul has a majestic Catholic cathedral, the state capitol and some handsome old buildings and broad tree-lined avenues of mansions.

Minneapolis has much glass and steel, and prominent among its shining towers of commerce are the IDS Tower, the skyscraper of the plains, and the striking Federal Reserve Bank. The theatre founded by Sir Tyrone Guthrie as a mid-Western seed-bed and oasis of art is part of the way in which Minneapolis mixes pleasure with its business. The city is one of the world's great wheat markets and is a flour-milling and creamery centre. In the grain exchange, where bids have to be made by public outcry, groups of men press close to each other and bellow their offers at the tops of their voices in bedlamic fury. It is much more peaceful in Minnehaha park where, as Longfellow wrote in his *Song of Hiawatha*:

> ...the Falls of Minnehaha
> Flash and gleam among the oaktrees,
> Laugh and leap into the valley.

The falls are there still, and you might imagine the arrow-maker and his dark-eyed daughter...

> From the waterfall he named her,
> Minnehaha, Laughing Water.

Part of the elegance of Minneapolis is its lakes. There are eleven in the city, clean enough to swim in; and in the winter they resemble Brueghel paintings, dotted with skaters and skiers. Lakes are part of Minnesota's wild grandeur. The state licence plates carry the motto: Minnesota: 10,000 Lakes; but, depending at what stage a large puddle or a little pond qualifies as a lake, there are reckoned, by some counts, to be fifteen thousand; a lovely legacy of the ice age glaciers which carved them.

The part of St Paul where I lived had a small-town atmosphere. I lived in a college room, close by Summit Avenue. Scott Fitzgerald lived on this avenue for a while, and when he had written the last word of *This Side of Paradise* he ran down the pavement shouting: 'It's done. It's finished!' My room looked out on to red brick Victorian college buildings, mature trees and constantly scampering unshy squirrels. The neighbourhood had a genteel air. The houses were spacious and set back in avenues of trees; though some of the elms had the dreaded Dutch pox, and those marked for felling were daubed with crosses, like doors in the Black Death.

One or two of our group, reflecting on our college life and the lectures we attended on politics and history, felt they were back to being students again and grumbled about it. But I had never been a student before and I enjoyed it, reinforcing my belief that further education is wasted on people in their twenties because they are not old enough to savour it. Anyway, there was a lot to do, and, like spoilt children, we had plenty of treats. One sunny day we all boarded a luxurious cabin cruiser for a swan down the river. The boat was owned by a genial man called Art, and it was a proper gin palace with a bar, television, furry bunks and carpeted walls, and a large organ. Art sat down at this, a modern Captain Nemo, and played jolly tunes of yesteryear as the Mississippi slid beneath our keel.

While in the college we were the long-term guests of American families. A number of brave souls had agreed to take a journalist under their wing, entertain him to a meal from time to time, take him out on social occasions and give him an insight into American family life and social mores. As most of these hosts came complete with children the journalist was also able to get a view of Young America and Very Young America. The hosts chose each journalist before his arrival in America by studying a list. A pin would have worked just as well. The system is a gamble (occasionally a host and journalist hate each other on sight), but somehow it works most of the time. It says something about the American generosity and willingness to gamble.

I was most fortunate with my own hosts, a college lecturer and a newspaper executive. Their wives proved constantly that there is such a thing as real and delicious food in America, and they pandered to the passion I developed for wild rice, a grain harvested by Indians in northern Minnesota. I was taken to dinners, concerts and the theatre, watched television with the kids and was lent cars and skis and, on one occasion, a house. I was invited, though not pressed, to go to church and to indulge in the sub-religion of jogging. It all works because Americans are genuinely hospitable and are experienced and good at entertaining. The layer of reserve found in Britain is shallower in America. Provided he knows he is not being exploited the American is happy to give. Your comfort is his concern. It is something that goes right through the social scale and it is one of the best strands in the American fabric.

Meanwhile, back on the campus, we were able to observe Young America at its studies. The only eccentric thing the students did was to join the college pipe band, an extra-ordinary transplant, whose members wore kilts and sporrans and could be found playing bagpipes at college ceremonies, reminding me of a twelfth-century Welsh poet's description of piping:

> The churl did blow a grating shriek,
> The bag did swell, and harshly squeak.

Otherwise the students seemed to grit their teeth braces and work hard. And in that they were like most of the college people we met. Less than a decade before, their predecessors were on the march in many parts of the United States — against the war in Vietnam, for civil rights, for freedom of all kinds. The campuses everywhere were in turmoil. Students were a central part of the great upheaval, the shout at what was perceived as the indifference, cynicism and corruption of America. The frightened adults and authorities of that decade, unable to cope with the anger and fearful of where it might lead, sent in soldiers who tear-gassed their children and, here and there, shot them. In America, always, the gun.

I met people who had been students in those years and who had been profoundly affected by what they experienced. Their pride in what they did, the protesting and marching, remains strong. They felt they had helped to make America a more decent place. The students I met, however, had been ten years

14

old, maybe younger, when all that was going on. For many of them, it seemed, the war, Watergate, civil rights, the whole critique of the American young, was recessed in history. Most of the young people I met in colleges seemed conservative and exercised primarily by their studies, anxious for good diplomas and qualifications to fit them for good and well-paid jobs. Vietnam and the corruption of the executive were to many of them already misted by the years. Perhaps that is too sweeping a generalization, but teachers said to me that today's students were much more like those in the 1950s, studies-oriented and less interested than the aberrant Sixties generation in issues of conscience and society. Some of them thought it a pity. Others thought it a return to proper American standards.

When winter set in, the cold was colder than most of us had ever known. The snow was powdery and the air dry, but the cold was exhilarating and my feet never grew to be chilled slabs as they do in Britain.

The first thing that happens when you step out on a winter's morning is that the hairs in your nostrils freeze. I found that my camera would be good for only two or three exposures before the shutter froze. The temperature in St Paul can fall to the minus thirties and it averages one hundred and sixty days a year of freezing, or below freezing, temperatures. I felt sorry for those Africans and Asians in our party who had never even seen snow before. Although Americans were at that time making a lot of noise, rather guiltily, about using too much energy and there was much talk about saving it, I found that the central heating temperature in most buildings, especially public ones, was unbearable. I turned the radiators off in my room and the ambient heat was quite enough. I didn't have to go out for a meal: I could telephone the local pizza shop and the pizza van would come out on its mission of mercy.

Minnesotans take a determined stand, at times an almost fiendish pleasure, in fighting winter and keeping life as normal as possible. Winter is the expected enemy, to be conquered and, whenever possible, enjoyed. So windows and walls are insulated and the roads are kept clear by continuous ploughing. The airport, too, is kept open in the fiercest weather. In the centre of Minneapolis the main office and shopping blocks are connected by the skyway system, a network of enclosed and heated pedestrian links high above the streets. For the fortunate and well-organized it is possible to drive to and from work, and spend a working day, complete with lunch and some shopping, without stepping on to snow or breathing the freezing outside air. When they are not beating the snow, Minnesotans are playing in it. They positively gambol. They like to go cross-country skiing, which is a kind of high-speed shuffling, and is not only exhilarating, as I discovered, but burns up calories like paper in a furnace. And in rural parts they buzz around on snowmobiles. These are motorbikes on skis and are very noisy and often crash into trees. They were invented partly to enable people to move swiftly and spectacularly over snowy terrain, and also to enable men to show off while their lady passengers hug them tightly in terror. They are thus favoured by the young and by late developers.

Minnesotans take such pride in their ability to prepare for winter, deal with it and enjoy it with a hedonistic delight, that they are rather contemptuous of their fellow Americans in more southerly states who find themselves overwhelmed by unusual severe weather. Minnesotans enjoy switching on the evening television news and watching, say, the people of Little Rock up to their ears in snow and normal life brought to a stop: at such times Minnesota is almost unbearably smug.

The British interest in weather, part of our national image, is rather small compared with the devoted attention Americans pay to their weather and weather forecasting. Television weathermen have toothy smiles and sharp suits and a line in patter that fits their status as stars, and they are featured strongly in their television station's promotions. Many of them also get the swollen salaries of those who float in television's stratosphere. To me, a newcomer, it seemed that talk about weather occupied an inordinate amount of air time; but then America often experiences most dramatic and extreme weather. The cold is colder, the heat hotter. And there are other hazards, like tornadoes and hurricanes. Americans talk far more about the weather than we do; but they have more weather to talk about.

I used to hear much weather talk — and stories of blizzard-trapped motorists saving themselves by tearing out the car seat stuffing for insulation — at lunches, dinners, receptions and parties. Along with my colleagues I was invited to so many of these that I felt we had been elected to the International Society of Freeloaders. Because we were exotics our hosts were interested in our countries; and, being Americans, and Americans have a great desire to be loved, they were also deeply interested in what we thought of them.

I soon learnt from early conversation that Vietnam was still a raw wound and that the healing process would be a long one. Some people found it almost impossible to discuss. The war had left them with a profound sense of shame, of disgust, so that the mention of the war was too painful for them and they side-stepped and talked of something else or went to get another drink. For many Americans, indeed, Vietnam, I found, was a taboo subject, rather like death. I sometimes felt that I was intruding in private grief. For some people the war and what it meant still has to be explained. After the First World War European poets spent years writing about the pain of that disaster, trying to come to terms with it; and Americans are beginning to approach what at first seems unapproachable, too tender to touch, through films and books. If many endure the pain in private, or push the whole experience deeper in their minds, hoping to bury it, there are others who react to the word Vietnam with a sudden fierce pride and defiance. They splutter about crazy liberals and students, the campus bums as President Nixon called them, cheating the United States of victory in its just crusade against evil.

'Damn, we were made to fight with one hand tied behind our backs. If it hadn't been for those politicians we could have finished it off.'

In a small town in the mid-West a man remembered the youth who had gone off to the war and had been the first from the town to be killed. 'Some folks were almost proud that we'd lost a boy and they compared him with the boys they read about who'd dodged the draft. But after a time people began to feel uneasy. We wondered what we were doing sending our kids out there. Sure the kid was brave. But what was it for? It's one thing to lose a boy in a war you are certain is right and just. It's another to lose one when you feel uncertain and guilty.'

An army officer reacted sharply in a conversation when the word defeat was mentioned. 'It wasn't defeat. We could have finished the job. We could have smashed them. We didn't lose. It was simply that we lost the war at home. So we withdrew.'

A young man who went to Vietnam said: 'I'm still trying to come to terms with it. The war turned all our ideas upside down. I went with a sense of duty and came back with a sense that it was all a mistake. And when I came back I found that people didn't want to talk about it. When men came back from the Second World War they were heroes and everybody wanted to hear their stories. But some of our guys were sneered at when they got back. And I find I can only talk about the war in private with other guys who went. Lots of people dodged the draft and they still get stick from the older people. And draft-dodgers are looked on by other people as boys who did the right thing. And maybe they did. People are still confused and split. Lots of folks got used to being part of a country that always won and they just can't come to terms with losing.'

Defeat and withdrawal remain an almost unbearable injury; and for other Americans the shame of involvement is almost unspeakable. An era, a national outlook and confidence in experts, were buried in Vietnam, and Americans are only just beginning to talk it out. I formed the impression that Vietnam was a subject better talked of in private, not raised in certain circles, always approached with care. The very word seemed sometimes to have the effect of an expletive and its ripples washed uncomfortably around the room.

5

I liked to watch the college students at their exotic breakfasts. Sure enough they sloshed syrup over their pancakes and over bits of thin charred bacon. Most American bacon is murdered; there is a long tradition of violence to bacon in America. They poured from a great range of coloured, popping, crackling nursery cereals and chose from several kinds and colours of milk. They would take two or three doughnuts from a pile and trawl them through a chocolate dip, then coat them with hundreds-and-thousands, and wash them down with Coca-

Cola, or something similar. Every morning they would eat a dentist's nightmare.

Food for many American children is a kind of dietary adventure playground. The variety of it is surprising to a visitor's eyes, and so is the quantity available and thrown away as waste. Obesity is a considerable problem in the United States or, to put it another way, there are a lot of fat kids. There are lots of fat adults, too, and one American in four is said to be overweight.

For parents there is an answer, apart from the obvious one: in the small ads of the *National Geographic Magazine*, and other publications, are advertisements for special camps where boys and girls aged eight and over may be sent to lose weight. 'Boys eight to eighteen lose twenty to fifty pounds and have the time of your life,' they say. 'Year-round counselling helps maintain weight loss.'

It is hardly surprising that many Americans consume too much. Food is manifestly abundant, relatively cheap and attractively advertised. It is served up in many restaurants and fast-food places in Technicolor fashion, with all manner of sploshed sauces and relishes, salads, odds and ends and comforting nursery drinks. There are far more restaurants per hundred mouths than there are almost anywhere in the world, and Americans take at least a third of their meals in restaurants.

Because Americans like to know exactly what they are getting, restaurateurs have had to become lyricists of the menu, and dishes tend to be described down to the last grain of salt, and sometimes with a dash of whimsy. Thus:

'This is the slam-dunk of pizza eaters. Catch this, no less than thrice-risen dough, rich homemade red sauce, olive oil, sautéed fresh onions, green peppers, fresh champagne-cork-sized mushrooms, a special blend of cheeses and a modest smile of approval from the cook.'

And: 'Picture our Millburger smothered in mushrooms and sautéed onions, topped with melted cheese and capped with tomato slices. Now envision that nestled in a platter of hot French fries or breaded mushrooms beside a cool, crisp salad. That's it. You've just fantasized what you can realize by suggesting we build you a Deluxe Millburger Platter.'

19

For their routine meals many Americans are content to do without that kind of gifted script-writing. With time short because they are working or travelling they like to take in their food in the manner of bombers taking on fuel in mid-air. It is only one step away from intravenous feeding. They scoop up a hamburger and masticate it quickly. The hamburger is the quintessential fast meal and has not yet been proved to damage health. The national hamburger chains have made their fortunes by cooking billions of beef buns very quickly, and ensuring that the hamburger tastes the same and is served in exactly the same way wherever you are in the United States. The most awe-inspiring hamburger I ever attempted was a double-heroburger. It looked like a boxing glove, and after I had eaten it I felt as if I had been hit by one.

The sandwich is something the Americans have made their own. It is bigger and better than the British sandwich, which is pathetic by comparison, and is offered in infinite variety and swiftly gobbled.

The bolting of food was noticed by Charles Dickens when he was in America nearly one hundred and forty years ago. 'The custom of hastily swallowing large quantities of animal food, three times a day, and rushing back to sedentary pursuits after each meal, must be changed.'

Well, it hasn't. The habit is ingrained. At lunchtime especially only a minority of Americans eat in the European or Asian fashion, making an occasion of meals, eating at reasonable speed, enjoying conversation and sipping wine. (And Californian wine is excellent.) I imagine that the custom of chopping up food first, before shovelling it with a fork, evolved as a time-saver. And Americans are time-conscious. Generally speaking, they start work earlier than we do, lunch around noon, and have their dinner around six. The work ethic is strong. I once went to a working lunch with some businessmen, which meant we ate sandwiches and talked. They were self-righteous about their prandial heroism, but I formed the view that it was barbaric and a cause of ulcers. I have to be fair, though, and say that I went to many business lunches where there was proper food on a plate, and people told me that lunch was becoming a more relaxed meal. It seems that more Americans are deciding, even if reluctantly, that if they have to eat they might as well enjoy it.

One of the favourite eating places is the cinema. Americans usually stock up in the foyer with a good supply of hamburger, chocolate, a pint of Coke and a cardboard bucket, as big as a deck pail, full of popcorn. I am sure the sound track is turned up to drown the sound of squelching mastication. A lot of popcorn is dropped and I often found it difficult to leave a cinema at the end of the film because my shoes were glued to the floor by sticky popcorn. I suppose that sometimes people have to go home in their socks.

6

As with food, so with the motor-car in America. Big steaks, big cars. On the table and in the restaurant, on the road and in the parking lot, you could always see the fat evidence of plenty. Yummy, soft, squashy, bright, sweet cartoon food and soft, squashy, bright, shiny fat comic-strip cars, combined in abundance in the land of milk and petrol to gratify senses, appetites, dreams and egos.

The motor-car, ever-present prop on the American stage, is part of American swagger and exuberance. In all its generously proportioned forms the car has been an indispensable part of the American dream and expectation. Indeed, so central is it to the way of life, so much a keystone of culture, of work and play and courtship — the back seat of the car was for two generations the hymeneal altar of America — that it is surprising that the right of the people to bear ignition keys and drive vehicles freely in the pursuit of the full and abundant life is not enshrined in the constitution.

Americans emerge from the womb groping for a steering wheel. In Los Angeles, where the automobile has made legs obsolete, you can be stopped by the police and questioned if you are found walking in a residential district: shanks's pony is considered a suspicious steed. An inability to drive is considered positively un-American, and a man without either driving licence or credit cards would be considered a subversive. It is no wonder that in a country where walking has never been fashionable, where the automobile is so central to the economy and the national life, that when businessmen gathered for lunch in Detroit, the motor-car capital of the United States, the grace said before the meal was this:

'Almighty God, we thank thee for the wheel, for the person who made it into a vehicle, for those who produce it, and bless us who use it. Amen.'

By Ford!

The roads of America, especially the interstate highway network begun in the 1950s and now being completed, have opened up the country to almost everyone. I found that driving in America is a more enjoyable experience than at home. Petrol is cheaper, the roads are less congested and the highway on a clear and pleasant day can be an entertainment. The lower speed limit means that driving is far less competitive and more relaxed than in Britain: you arrive fresher. Americans have a greater familiarity with cars and their lane discipline is good. They make room and cruise like large and amiable dogs, while Britons, in comparison, are snappy and anxious terriers. 'Drive Friendly', say the roadsigns in Texas; and many Americans do. Occasionally they shoot or stab each other over real or imagined slights on the highway, but that is because the threshold of violence is lower in the United States; in general, driving does not occupy such an important part in the puerile ideas of masculinity and self-esteem as it does in Britain and other parts of the world. Americans do not feel the same need to prove themselves at the wheel; and in a country where there is bullish snorting and pawing at the ground in other areas of life, I found the relative tolerance and low boiling-point in driving a paradox.

The national speed limit of fifty-five miles an hour has reduced the number of accidents considerably, as well as saving petrol. Until the limit was imposed the death and injury toll was very high. The beneficial effects of the limit coincided with an improvement in car design following the attack on the American car industry by Ralph Nader. His *Unsafe at Any Speed*, published in 1965, accused the manufacturers of putting profits and style in front of safety. It led to safety legislation and a reform of ideas in the motor industry.

As many Americans told me, they used to drive at eighty or ninety miles an hour. A few told me they would still like to do so. In the west, where, perhaps, *machismo* and rugged independence are more important qualities than in the east, some men regard the speed limit as an irksome imposition of authority and an interference by the central government in God-given state rights and Ford-given motoring rights.

'Speed limit's plumb crazy.' a Texan said. 'They just sit on their butts in Washington thinkin' they know best. Hell, they got no distance to drive home or to drive to work. But it's big down here and we've got to go faster.'

'Interferin' with our rights. They don't know nothing about our roads out west,' a man said in Wyoming, where the people were thinking at the time of defying the government and driving just as fast as they liked.

A lot of signs beside the highways warn: 'Fifty-five means fifty-five.' And the law in most states is firmly enforced. Determined lawbreakers can fit their cars with a radar detector which tells them when a radar-equipped police car is in the vicinity. 'Fuzzbuster — Untraps Radar!' The police have another weapon up their sleeves, however. They monitor traffic from aircraft and warn on the signs: 'Speed Checked by Aircraft.' And, mischievously: 'Smile — You're On Radar!'

On the interstate highways many drivers watch the behaviour of the enormous lorries which are the kings of the road. Lorry drivers often like to exceed the speed limit a little and they have to keep their wits about them and their eyes peeled. They communicate with each other by way of citizens' band radio which is as difficult for a stranger to penetrate as is Cockney rhyming slang. In this argot the police are known as Smokeys, or Bears. A police station is known as a Bear Cave, and a policewoman as a Mama Bear. A highway is a Super Slab, and while they are on it the drivers look out for Bears in the Air (police aircraft), X-rays (radar), County Mounties (county police). If it is Clean (no police in view), they Drop the Hammer (accelerate), but keep on the alert for Fluff Stuff (snow), Window Washer (rain), Willy Weavers (drunk drivers) and Harvey Wallbangers (reckless drivers). If they are unlucky they might be stopped by a Plain Wrapper (unmarked police car) and ordered to Feed the Bears (pay a fine). Apart from Bears, many lorry drivers who take a chance and carry an overweight load to make more money, have to avoid Chicken Coops (weighing stations) where police and weight inspectors are ready to enforce the strict load laws. Warned by radio of Chicken Coops, drivers with fat loads take off along minor roads to avoid them.

A driver without Ears (radio) has to do as the lorries do. If they are keeping to the speed limit they have been alerted that there are Wall to Wall Bears in the area.

One fine morning, on a road in Minnesota, Ear-less and a shade careless, I allowed my speed to creep up and, too late, noticed an aubergine-coloured car of the Minnesota State Patrol coming towards me. When it had passed I looked in the mirror and saw it braking and turning, leaning over squashily as it made its U, then coming up behind me with red lights flashing. I was put in mind of Broderick Crawford's opening remarks in *Highway Patrol*, which was one of the earliest American pap-drama series on British television: 'Whenever the laws of any state are broken, a duly authorized organization swings into action. It may be called the State Police, the Rangers, or the Highway Patrol. These are the men whose daring, skill and courage enforce and preserve our state laws.'

I stopped and got out and the state trooper glanced quickly at my hands to ensure that I was unarmed. Irritated drivers have been known to shoot traffic cops, as they might swat a fly. He invited me into his car. I sat behind his high-powered rifle in its upright holster and saw that his radar had recorded my speed at sixty-five. The trooper was genial.

'Guess you can't deny you've committed an offence, but this time it's a warning,' he said. 'Fifty-five is the limit, so hold it down to under sixty, or next time it's dollars.' He gave me the warning ticket and waved me out. 'Have a good day!'

A friend of mine from Wales was once stopped for speeding in America. He smartly noticed that the officer's name tag on his uniform said Jones. Trying to curry favour he said: 'Jones, eh, with a name like that you must have Welsh blood.'

'That's right sir,' the patrolman said. 'Welsh on my daddy's side and Scottish on my Ma's. And it's the Scottish side that's giving you this ticket.'

My friend paid a fine of eleven dollars on the spot and later mentioned the incident in passing to his dinner hosts. 'Hell, you didn't pay the fine did you?' they grumbled. 'Oh well, leave it to us. We know the people in charge round here. We'll fix it for you.' Sure enough, when he returned to Wales, there was a cheque for eleven dollars waiting for him. In America, a little gentle fixing of that kind is not universally held to be deplorable.

On a long drive you can collect educating little bits of America because Americans are great labellers. They like being told what to do and what is going on. The custom of labelling people began here, and almost everyone who works behind a counter, who serves and meets the public in some way, has his name on his chest. If an American sees a space he likes to fill it with a sign or notice, even if the message is otiose. But the signs are often entertaining, sometimes charming.

Your Friendly Dixie Store. If You Can't Stop, Wave.

Car Wash. All Beige Cars Ten Dollars Discount Today.

We Aspire to Inspire The Squire to Acquire The Attire That Damsels Admire.

Welcome to Gardendale. Nice People Live Here.

Fire Dept. Turkey Shoot.

I liked to collect the little nuggets of information and state pride encapsulated in the licence plates of passing cars. Arizona: Grand Canyon State. Arkansas: Land of Opportunity. Alabama: Heart of Dixie. Illinois: Land of Lincoln. Mississippi: Hospitality State. Tennessee: Volunteer State. Delaware: The First State. Minnesota: 10,000 Lakes. Wisconsin: America's Dairyland. New Mexico: Land of Enchantment. Florida: Sunshine State. Pennsylvania: Keystone State. Louisiana: Bayou State. Montana: Big Sky. North Carolina: First in Freedom. New Jersey: Garden State. Washington DC: Nation's Capital.

A lorry comes thundering by and shows you its back on which is the angry message: This Vehicle Pays Three Thousand Dollars A Year Taxes. And a trafficade, as they say, of funeral cars swishes up the highway, following the flashing orange beacon of the cortège leader.

On the radio, as it happens, a man from the Jones Funeral Home is solemnly reading brief obituaries to a background of doleful organ music.

'Presented as a public service by the Jones Funeral Home. We take time to do the little things. Plan for the inevitable. Jones Funeral Home.' There is a brief burst of news in gobbets of about ten seconds, interspersed with commercials; and then: 'That news was brought to you by the Overhead Door Company.'

The roads are clean all over America. There are signs warning: 'Driver Subject To Arrest For Litter Thrown From Vehicle.' And 'Littering Is Filthy So Don't Do It.' It is another paradox. Americans happily litter their towns and the roads leading into towns with a hideous jumble of advertising, but, unlike the dirty British, they do not throw their cans, newspapers, bags and ashtray contents onto the roads.

Although, through jogging and the growth of sport, Americans have rediscovered legs, they still like to live in their cars a lot. The drive-in cinemas, the great centres of auto-eroticism, are, apparently, beginning to decline in popularity but they remain an important aspect of American culture; and so are the drive-in restaurants. The words drive-in restaurant are surely a contradiction in terms: but no. You drive up to a menu and a microphone stuck on a stick, and call your order into it. The food is delivered by short-skirted waitresses and comes complete with those sachets of ketchup which, when opened, squirt bloodily on to your knee and the car radio.

The best drive-in fun is drive-in banking because it does not seem like banking at all. You drive up to the window, pop your travellers' cheque into a sliding, bullet-proof mechanical hand and speak over a microphone to a pretty and cutely uniformed girl. On her chest is a badge telling you she is called Sherryl or Pattie-Anne and she has a nice bright smile. Out pops a bright little envelope which contains your money — and a couple of candy-striped sweets to fill that awkward gap between the between-meal snacks. And, as with money, so with God. You can also pray in drive-in churches where the minister relays in honeyed tones the word of the Lord from a gallery. The congregation is spared the trouble of kneeling and standing and receives the little gobbets of religion and well-being as if from an aerosol.

Today, however, the American is having to reconsider his relationship with the motor-car. It is one of the momentous readjustments of history. The realization that petrol is finite has chilled spines in the manner of rumours and rumbles of an approaching plague. No wonder some people have panicked and reached for their six-shooters and have threatened and killed for petrol. A key pillar of a mighty culture has been shaken.

The talk is of saving and scaling down, the kind of talk that only a few years ago would have been regarded as unAmerican, unpatriotic. Americans have always said that they need brontosaurian cars because they drive long distances and must have the comfort that only large cars provide. But this is disingenuous. Americans may drive long distances on holiday, but I would guess that most of them commute no further than most Europeans; and if they have a long way to go they fly. They know that comfort is not related to size only, but has to do with design, springing, soundproofing and the science of ergonomics.

The fact is that Americans have always liked large cars because their tradition has been large cars, and large cars suit their ideas about themselves. The befinned and heavily chromed guzzlers of petrol have always symbolized an age of plenty and a way of living.

Evidently the years of excess are over. American cars are like flabby businessmen being pushed, on doctor's orders, on to a régime of carrot juice and steam baths. In Detroit, where Fords showed me their slimmer, petrol-pinching new models being banged and screwed together on their relentless production lines, executives were grumbling a bit about meeting government demands for more economical cars. They thought the demands strict; and they were squeaking a little with the pain of changing habits ingrained for more than half a century. There has never been a tradition of compact car design in America. Until recently the designers have had to do little more than go to the drawing-board and make a few broad sweeps to satisfy a motoring public which wanted its cars big and powerful. Very few American cars have been elegant in the way that European cars have been: the best of them have achieved an imposing appearance of power and sleekness, perhaps a hint of grandeur here and there, and often a bulky opulence. But it is only in the past two or three years that designers have had to begin their revolution and draw cars with an eye to economy, compactness and the considerations of aerodynamics. The cumbersome fore and aft overhangs are being chopped off, the first transverse engines are being installed and great chunks of metal are being reduced. The American car is no longer going to be the medieval armoured horse it once was. A somewhat sprightlier sort of war pony is emerging.

Of course, the designers cannot please everyone. A petrol station proprietor, filling the tank of a new and fairly small Detroit-built car I had rented, looked carefully at the machine and gave his verdict. 'Well, it's a good little car all right. But just look at the design. It's European. Hell, we're letting foreigners get away with everything in this country. Seems to me that everything I see these days is designed or built by foreigners. Why can't we do anything for ourselves any more?'

While car manufacturers are having to bend to the winds, and the public goes through its uncomfortable re-education, there will no doubt always be some demand for the great battlewagons and limousines, as American as the stars and stripes, beloved of company chairmen, entertainers and criminals. The motor men fervently hope so. And everybody is hoping that latter-day alchemists will somehow render sunbeams and chicken-dung into a miracle fuel.

'Life without the motor car is just unthinkable for most Americans,' a friend reflected as we cruised an interstate in quiet comfort. 'It's not just a matter of transport and freedom and things like that. Life is so hectic for many people, so crowded and noisy and pressured, that the motor car is like a refuge, a sort of chapel, a place for quiet reflection. Dammit, it's the only place where many of us can be alone.'

7

An American said: 'I think your British newspapers are disgusting. They print pictures of naked girls. That's shocking. We'd never stand for that in America.'

Nor would they. American newspapers are decent and wholesome and bottoms and bosoms have they none. And most of them censor out even mild swear words, like d**n. Murdochism, which made breasts a central selling and packaging feature of British newspapers, would not be tolerated by mainstream newspaper readers in America whose attitudes are conditioned to a greater extent by religion and modesty. Page Three would be burnt in the streets of middle America.

When the television drama *Holocaust* was screened in Britain there was a harrowing scene of women entering a gas chamber. In the United States the scene was priggishly edited because the women were naked.

And there was a rare brouhaha over the case of the naked cheerleaders. Cheerleaders are comely girls who appear at football matches to stimulate enthusiasm for their teams. They march and prance like liberty horses and twirl batons and frazzle pompoms about to keep the fans cheering. Cheerleading began in colleges, but now a lot of professional teams have their own platoons of cheerleaders. The Dallas Cowboys, for example, have a cheerleader team called the Cowgirls, while the Los Angeles Rams call theirs the Embraceable Ewes.

The cheerleaders represent an ideal in young American womanhood. They have lovely legs and what is known as a good figure. They have large mouths and constant bright white smiles and flowing hair. They are essentially wholesome and winsome clean-living girls who love their Mamas and Daddies and go to church on Sunday.

And they have cute names to fit their cuteness, names as sweet as chocolate doughnuts, such as the names of the Junior Misses, the outstanding high school girls of America, who, in 1978, were called: LuAnn, JerriDee, JoAnne, Jaxie, Shelley, Tammy, Candy, Becky, Lady Lyn, Marlys and Cyndi.

Imagine the shock, then, when it was discovered that one of the San Diego Chargettes, the cheerleaders of the San Diego Chargers, had posed birthday-suited for *Playboy*. Feeling that the wholesome girl-next-door image of the entire cheerleading team had been damaged, the football club sacked the lot. Other clubs who found that some of their girls had posed naked for magazines also gave them their cards. In this crisis, the National Football League was asked to comment, but could only say: 'There isn't any league position on nudity.'

All this may look like prudishness, but it is another of the paradoxes. The cheerleaders are, in a sense, presented as beautiful and virginal; but they tend to wear exiguous costumes which are meant to give men an eyeful. The same sort of costume is almost a uniform forced on innocent and long-suffering waitresses and barmaids throughout the United States. In hotels, restaurants, fast-food places and bars you can be served by girls wearing anachronistic Playboy Bunny leotards — a curious relic of 1950s glamour — or very short skirts or bare midriffs. Americans have no sense of place or occasion about this. A bottom is fine, but in its place. I was particularly irritated once when a waitress's short-skirted bottom tangled with the jungly foliage of my Bloody Mary and knocked it over, an accident which only attracted several more bottoms, bearing cloths.

There used to be a convention in Hollywood films that scenes ended either at the bedroom door or, if they went into the bedroom, propriety was maintained if actors and actresses in bed kept one foot on the floor. Dressing the way they do, cheerleaders and tutu'd waitresses make an appeal to the red-bloodedness of American males, while keeping a foot on the floor. Once they drop the final veil they are in breach of the puritan ethic and must go.

Today that ethic seems a sandcastle in an advancing tide. In a few years pornography has become one of the great industries of America. It is estimated that pornographic films earn more than four thousand million dollars a year, which is as much as the conventional film industry and the record industry combined. The ten leading magazines in which nudity and sex are important or sole features have a monthly circulation of sixteen million. Bookshops and peepshows are especially profitable: a large one in New York is said to make ten thousand dollars a day. Peepshow slot machines offer short segments of cheaply-made film, and there are shops where the customers put in their money in such quantities that the machines have to be emptied into buckets every two hours and the money hurried to the bank. It is a far cry from the time, not so long ago, when the Los Angeles education authority banned Tarzan books because Tarzan and Jane were not married.

8

One night I went to a concert and sat close to a television

camera set up in the aisle. The operator of it was a tall girl wearing the usual earphones; and she had on a smart long black evening dress. Her ensemble put me in mind of the BBC in its Reith Age, when radio announcers and news readers went to the microphone in dinner jackets. I mentioned this to my neighbour. He looked at the girl and said: 'She must be Public Broadcasting.'

For an increasing number of Americans, Public Broadcasting is the saving grace of their television system. It stands for a certain quality; an island in the engulfing pap. I was surprised to find so many Americans embarrassed by the bulk of what is on their screens, surprised by the vehemence of the contempt so many young people and children have for it. With the rueful faces of parents who constantly have to apologize for the delinquency of a wilful child, people would say: 'We sure hope you don't judge us by our television.'

It is a commonplace for British visitors to America to say how bad American television is, and so stand in agreement with American critics. But American television springs from a different culture and broadcasting tradition. Criticism of it brings us to the large and controversial question of what 'good' television is and who defines it. Given the voracious nature of the medium and the conditions in which it exists in the United States it is hardly possible for it to be 'good' continuously, whatever the standard applied. In any case, it is easy for people from Britain to be complacent: we tend to ignore the element of third-rate television we have at home, and the amount of American material used as makeweight.

Yet what the British visitor constantly hears is praise of the BBC. 'Ah, the BBC,' Americans say respectfully, as if intoning a sacred word. 'If only we had the BBC.' Actually, they do have the BBC, and the pick of British independent television too. So the dramas, melodramas and documentaries which keep Britons nailed to their Parker Knolls also transfix Americans. Bearing in mind the nature of some of the most popular series, like *The Forsyte Saga* and *Upstairs, Downstairs*, Americans are left with a fond, off-centre view of dear old Britain. Nevertheless the impact of British television on American television serves to make stark the difference in quality between the two. British programmes look original, crisper, better produced. The home product looks soggy, amateurish, unimaginative, loud and inconsequential.

The differences lie in tradition and purpose. British broadcasting began as an institution and grew under the leadership of people devoted to a concept of broadcasting as a public service, educator and medium of truth and good things. It built a reputation for honesty and quality. The introduction of commercial television blew welcome breezes; but even the famous 'licences to print money' issued to its pioneers did not dilute the central tradition of broadcasting, especially as far as news, documentary and drama were concerned.

American television, like radio, began in the American way, as a gold rush. In the same manner that the west was won, with rapid settlement of land, there was on the radio and television frontier a rapid settlement of air space. But, with some exceptions, broadcasting was not viewed as a public service and only a handful of people had the sort of ideas that shaped British television. Reith was a million miles away.

Indeed, radio and television in the United States were developed essentially as platforms for selling, and not with the aims of the broadcasting we are used to in Britain. American television shouts its wares and grabs attention and the prime concern among its moguls is programme popularity which is measured by the Nielsen ratings. Because popularity is connected with revenue these ratings are watched as closely as an electrocardiogram in an intensive care unit. The emphasis in programming is relentlessly down-market: inane quiz shows, lightweight soap opera, the gamut of slight programmes that can place burdensome time in the waste disposer. They tell us something about Americans, though. The quiz show contestants are uninhibited: they shriek and shake, show hysterical joy and deep grief, as they win and lose the fabulous trophies of conspicuous consumption. The eye-witnesses and people stopped in the streets for interviews are usually fluent and extrovert, with a gab gift rarely equalled in Britain. And some of the most popular shows are those in which audiences roar at amateur performers making fools of themselves.

As a medium of entertainment in the United States it fulfils its task: it is always there, like tap water. As a medium of education and enlightenment it is generally shallow and largely a failure. As a medium of information it is haphazard and usually merely cutaneous. As a medium of creativity it is in chains. And while it would be arguing too narrowly and mischievously to suggest that it is a dying medium, it is, in some respects, a puny and withered one.

This is a paradox, for what strikes the visitor, too, is its omnipresence and quantity. There are three giant networks, ABC, CBS and NBC, each with hundreds of affiliated stations throughout the country transmitting all day and much of the night. The scale of the commercialism is huge. Americans are used to it and they have probably developed a tolerance to commercials; perhaps even a need for them. At a film festival in Chicago there was a three-hour showing of advertisements said to be uninterrupted by programmes. Nevertheless I found the weight of commercials in American television oppressive and an important constituent in its narcotic quality. I felt like a French goose forced-fed with grain to make the liver swell; and I am certain that tests would show that American television makes you sleep more quickly than British television. The pace is bewildering. Not one half-second is wasted. The commercials come at furious speed. There is no decorous End of Part One caption between programme and advertisement — too wasteful. There is a sudden jump from *Ben Hur* into a bowl of crunchies. And the commercials are not usually well-made: they lack subtlety and humour and are simply crude sandwichboards of the air.

Because they call the tune they hamstring programme structure. They not only force interruptions, but in news and news magazine programmes, for example, they oblige presenters to speak the trailers that hint at the exciting things to come in the next segment; so that programmes often consist of advertisements and trailers and not much programme. And commercials make the watching of films on television maddening. Towards the denouement the commercials come smashing in increasingly frequently, so that you feel as angry as a baby snatched from the teat.

And, suddenly, in a news magazine, an interviewer will turn from the person he is interviewing and say to the camera: 'And now a commercial I recently recorded.' And there he is, large as life and twice as blatant, selling you Bloppo and insulting your intelligence. It struck me, when I saw it first, as a grotesque lack of integrity; but customs are different. Sponsors of televised football matches do not take the risk of having independent commentary on their games: they bring in their own commentators.

With some exceptions there is remarkable similarity between television front men and women, and this contributes to an overall blandness. With their similar hairstyles, clothing, faces and nowhere-in-particular voices, they all seem to have been sent to television stations by Central Casting. Some of the women, though, slip into stridency. Perhaps they feel they have to speak louder in what they perceive as a battle with men, so they read with chainsaw tones — a pity, because American English is at its most attractive when spoken firmly yet softly.

The reading is often done at a fair lick, too. Items are run one into the other and the newsreader is well into the second before you realize that he has finished the first. It is like meat emerging from the mincer. And sometimes there is a stream of information in printed form put on the screen which is quite different from what the reader is saying. It is supposed to double the information you receive, but it halves it. It sometimes seems, on American television, that there is a conspiracy against comprehension.

At the offices of CBS in New York I met some of the network's executives. They argued that, given the commercial framework in which television exists, there was not a lot wrong; that advertisements were the way in which television earned its living, that there was nothing wrong with being popular and entertaining millions. As for television journalism they pointed to their own CBS news, presented by Walter Cronkite, and to the quality of their weekly news magazine *60 Minutes*. They were right to do so: Mr Cronkite is everything that most American television isn't. He is good. He is avuncular and magisterial, the kind of institution that Richard Dimbleby was in Britain. He is integrity personified and has the authority that most presenters lack. Moreover, he reads and phrases in a way that makes what he says comprehensible. Mr Cronkite listened to what the executives said, but I felt he did not subscribe completely to their rather complacent view. He thought that good broadcasting journalism had a struggle to survive in the American system, and that there should be more time for news and explanation. As for *60 Minutes*, I thought it the best thing of its kind on commercial television, serious and professional, although it was patched by advertisements.

Radio and television are not entirely in the hands of commerce. There is also Public Broadcasting, which occupies a curious but increasingly important place in American mass communications. It is a minority channel, founded in 1967, and somehow survives on a mixture of inadequate government funding (there is no television licence), gifts from corporations and foundations, and some begging. Viewers who like it send in donations. Part of its appeal is that it is mercifully free of clutter: no commercials, none of the frenetic announcements and splutters that make most television painful. Its news and analysis are good and it shows a lot of British drama and dramatic series. It has more than two hundred and sixty stations throughout the country which supplement the national output with locally-made programmes, including ballets and concerts, dramas, debates. The stations act independently in this respect, putting out programmes to meet local needs.

Bill Kobin, chief of the Public Broadcasting station in Minneapolis–St Paul, said that commercial television was centralized, with decisions taken in New York. 'Public Broadcasting is a reaction against that centralization, a reaction too against the nature of commercial television. Many more people are wanting something better out of television. We try to give it. There's still a myth around that Public Broadcasting is geared to the well-educated élite, but that myth is crumbling because more people are catching on to what we offer and the audience gets increasingly broad. We experiment, too. We're the ones who show things like *Monty Python* and *The Prisoner*. We are more diverse than commercial television, and I think we have a sense of mission, certainly a feeling that we're doing something worthwhile. In commercial television journalistic standards have been eroded, and that is one reason why many top journalists just won't go into the medium. You get a show like *60 Minutes*, one of the highest-rated shows in the business, but there's not much else. Local news is usually entertainment and headlines and can't attract the best because it is too limited.'

Public Broadcasting is beset by money shortage and anxiety about future funding. 'If we had the money people would leave commercial television in droves to watch us,' Bill Kobin said. 'Somehow we have to have sounder funding.' It means that a balance will have to be struck between independent financing and government money: no one wants Public Broadcasting to be in the government's power, subject to the whim of politicians; and private financing is, in the end, variable and unreliable.

Nevertheless, more Americans are switching from commercial television, to the greater variety and stimulation of Public Broadcasting. There is no doubt that British programmes are a large part of the attraction, and this poses a dilemma. Funders are willing to support British material because it is so reliable: its very excellence, relatively speaking, means they are less inclined to put money into American-made programmes, often an unknown quantity and therefore a gamble.

Nobody believes that Public Broadcasting, and cable television which is also advertisement-free, will shake commercial television much in the next few years. But in offering even greater variety, they are part of a changing pattern in home entertainment. Instead of just sitting there, semi-comatose and inattentive, taking what is dished out, Americans will be making increasing use of cassettes, discs and video-recorders to make the box respond more to *their* desires. Although commercial television executives claim that audiences expect and want advertisements, people will have more avenues of escape. They won't have to resort to the measure that Elvis Presley once took when he could not stand something he saw on television. He shot the set.

I know the feeling.

9

A French writer once said that 'he who would know the heart and mind of America had better know football.' With this as a cue I stopped one Saturday morning in New Orleans to watch a football game. It was a little American vignette. The sun was shining and the scene was brightly coloured, noisy and innocently boisterous. The players wore bulbous helmets, face visors, mouthpieces, shoulder pads, kidney pads, spine pads, hip pads and grim looks. All this armour was bulging under gaudy royal blue and tangerine shirts, with large stripes and numbers; so that when they fell in a heap the players looked like carnival laundry falling out of a basket.

They were laying into each other, mauling, scrabbling, grunting and tumbling, like Trojans fresh out of the wooden horse and full of fight. But these combatants, so pugnacious and serious, were small boys aged seven and eight. All American footballers look grotesque in their armour, and anonymous in the shadowed recesses of their helmets; but these boys, because of their small stature, looked especially misshapen, like horrible little mutants in a science fiction film.

One of the teams was made up of black boys and the other of white. The black parents and friends were on one side of the field and the white crowd on the other. There was no rule about this and no animosity; it was just the way things were. There were a lot of dads there, shouting at the tops of their voices and running on to the field in the numerous stoppages to rub the bruised bodies of fallen sons. Mothers and sisters looked on with mingled pride, concern and excitement.

The intensity with which they followed the game is echoed and multiplied throughout the country. For football is one of America's greatest passions, an important aspect of its homogeneity and national language. President Nixon used to telephone football coaches for a chat: it was his way of trying to identify with ordinary Americans.

Some of its appeal lies in its violence, the crunch of bone and heaving weight of bodies as teams struggle for territory. It had its roots in colleges; and college football remains a mainstay of the game to this day. College matches are played in front of enormous crowds, are televised and are part of the sports monster created by commerce. Hundreds of young men get into colleges and earn their education on football scholarships: they enter college because they excel in a fierce and highly competitive game which embodies *machismo*, glamour and ruthless determination. It is also a game of critical timing, of great complexity, of teamwork; almost a bureaucracy of a game. It is played deadly seriously, and teams even pray for victory just before they leave the locker-room to meet their opponents. It is not often that sporting mania in Britain reaches the level it consistently reaches in the United States. Televised football has made millions addicts. Fans can watch several matches in a day, and the fat, glazed football junkie, slumped in a chair with his hand-held channel changer and his cans of Budweiser beer is one of the distinctive features of the social landscape of modern America.

The roughness of football, as I said, is part of its attraction. In the last century Harvard banned early versions of the game because of its wildness. In the 1880s the modern game was evolved from the British game of rugby football and new rules and styles of play gave the American game its singular character. In 1905 eighteen players were killed and more than one hundred and fifty injured, a score that led President Theodore Roosevelt to call for changes. Nevertheless the brutal element remains and so does the debate about it. I remember a newspaper series about violence on the field and a headline: 'The football helmet, meanest tool on earth' and an article headed: 'Ex-Ram loves football despite brain injury.'

The little lads I saw playing in New Orleans had started at the age of five or six. The outfits they were wearing had cost their dads about fifty pounds each. The protection was absolutely necessary, the fathers said, because football is a rough game. On the other hand, they said, it is a manly game and is good for boys. Elsewhere, though, I met many fathers, keen on sport themselves, who said they were discouraging their sons from playing the game because of its risks, because players were using their bodies as weapons. They felt that football had become too rough and that the standards of violence, even of terror, set in the professional game, and to a slightly lesser extent in the college game, were making football an ugly spectacle. They were, instead, encouraging their sons to play soccer, relatively new in America, but growing because it is safer, unarmoured and cheaper, its players get a greater share of the ball and it is more fluid.

The popular spectator sports in the United States are very big business and the major ones, like football and baseball, are thoroughly organized to meet the requirements of television and commerce. The top players earn huge salaries, up to three-quarters of a million dollars a year. The great opiates, television and football, are especially firmly wedged together. Clubs earn millions of dollars from television revenue — college football profits support other sports — and programme scheduling calls the tune. Football is deliberately stopped at intervals for the transmission of commercials. Because it is a game in which there are many natural stoppages this is not too difficult. But it is a problem with soccer. Its action is more continuous and it is not easy to find natural breaks for commercials, and having them at half-time is not enough. At the moment soccer and television do not need each other.

In terms of excitement, sport itself is not always enough. About football there is an atmosphere of media circus, a steady build-up to an emotional eruption. Baseball is rather more leisurely and social and has some of the aspects of cricket; and like cricket it stimulates sports writing of the finer sort. People move about and eat and drink, and before the seventh inning of the home team the crowd rises to its feet, then sits down, this quaint custom being known as the seventh inning stretch and considered good luck. If the ball is struck into the crowd the catcher keeps it as a souvenir. There is also an organist who plays mood music, rather like a cinema pianist in the days of silent films. When the mood is exciting he plays frantically and heralds dramatic moments with fanfares. In tense but lower-key moments he plays heavy background chords. Meanwhile giant electronic scoreboards throw up pithy captions and exhortations to 'Give him a big hand, folks!' Until I grew used to these artificial aids I found them comical.

For black people sport is a channel for advancement in a still discriminatory society. More than three-fifths of basketball players are black and the professional game is dominated by blacks and pays the highest average salaries, nearly ninety thousand pounds a year. More than two-fifths of footballers are black, though only a fifth of baseball players are. Nevertheless, black baseball players tend to be outstanding, though there is a tradition that they do not easily get to play in certain positions. For example there are very few black pitchers. The black presence in sport, and the success of many black sportsmen, is regarded by some people as evidence of the egalitarian nature of American society: talent wins through. On the other hand it gives a false idea of what success is. In sport, as in other fields, many aspire but few succeed, and for blacks the fall is harder and more disappointing. Reggie Jackson, a baseball superstar, once said: 'I am a black man with an IQ of a hundred and sixty, making seven hundred thousand dollars a year, and I still get treated like dirt.'

10

Even for English speakers the American language is not too difficult. The learning of it is something to enjoy. And the appreciation of it lies not only in vocabulary and in the way that Americans, in their loose-rein way, twist and bend their words and phrases. It also has much to do with the various sounds of American, the cadences, the differences of emphasis, the elisions; so that many words and phrases and pieces of writing are best spoken by Americans and cannot be well-said by anyone else — in much the same way that the full flavour of Irish, or Welsh or Scottish stories can only be extracted by a storyteller with the appropriate native accent. No Englishman, for example, can say 'Sure!' in the American fashion.

English pronunciation, in conversation with Americans, can bring home the point that Bernard Shaw wryly made about two countries separated by a common tongue. I remember the blank look I received the first time I used the word autumn in America.

'Pardon me?' was the mystified response.

'Autumn,' I repeated.

'I'm, sorry. I don't understand you.'

'Autumn,' I said, raising my voice in the usual manner of a man dealing with foreigners.

A long blank pause. And then a dawning comprehension.

'Ah — you mean — Oddm!'

Some of the vocabulary differences are well enough known — hood for car bonnet, elevator for lift, hogpen for pigsty, purse for handbag, instalment plan for HP, flashlight for torch, line for queue, faucet for tap; and so on. As I moved around the United States particles of American stuck to me as burrs to a sweater. A sodding contractor, for example, is not a botching builder, but a turf salesman. And pizzazz means glamour, gussied-up means dressed up and boffo means sensational.

Some of the meanings are plain enough, of course. Others a stranger can only guess at. Trawling through my memory for the words I heard and read in drugstores, on the campus and in Fatso's Diner, I come up with a sample which contains both categories: clambake, interstate, sourdough, skid row, slam dunk, John Doe, chuckwagon, woodchuck, gumbo, hound dog, precinct, mugwump, bankroll, honkytonk, redeye, home run, over easy, porkbarrel, caucus, stoop, mortician, bumbershoot, tenderize, prioritize, blueberry, gopher, picayune, levee, caboose, cookie, sub ... and so long. I once saw Distopia written as the antonym of Utopia. And I grew used to the solecistic use of the word momentarily, which has now come to mean soon — especially in telespeak. Thus: 'Our prográmme will return momentarily.'

Considering the plastic nature of their language and their exuberant irreverence for the rules, it is surprising that so many Americans work in a narrow verbal framework. 'Gee, that's really neat!' is the universal expression of approval; and poor old neat is hauled in to describe almost anything. In a really neat restaurant once I ate a really neat pizza and was told I had a really neat accent. In common with English on our side of the Atlantic, much American, especially the official and bureaucratic language, is not at all neat and is covered with a strangling ivy of jargon.

Nevertheless, enjoymentwise, there is much to be gained from listening to America talking. 'We Americans love to blab,' a professor of politics in Minnesota said to me. By and large I found that radio and television in the United States were poor mirrors of humour. Cartoonists and the humorists of newspapers and magazines are much closer to the national funny-bone and the interesting tributaries of conversation. Television, especially, projects a parrot-screeching aspect of humour; it is rarely droll. Mostly I picked up my bits of Americana in conversation enjoyed or overheard. A man once told me he had seen in that morning's paper an advertisement for a secondhand tombstone, for ten dollars — 'a bargain for anyone called Bailey'. It was humour of a gentle, leg-pulling sort that I encountered in many parts of America.

Of fragments of conversation overheard, my favourite is one I could not help hearing in a restaurant one evening. An intense young man was talking about himself, none too quietly, to a young woman whose hand he was holding over the table. He was relating, as they say, like mad; and gazing into her eyes he exclaimed: 'You must understand. I just happen to be brilliant and I've had to build my whole ego around that single fact.'

2
FIRST HAND

Pause by some neglected graveyard,
For a while to muse, and ponder
On a half-effaced inscription.
        Henry Wadsworth Longfellow

Into his right hand I placed mine. Here in this desolate bone-bare place, perhaps five thousand years before, he had chiselled out the shape of his splayed hand and then had patiently rubbed it smooth. I supposed that he had spent many months doing it, for this flat outcrop of pale rose-red quartzite is hard, and the tools employed for the task would have been simple stone ones. I knelt to place my hand in this reaching out-stretched hand fashioned so painstakingly. It fitted perfectly, the thumb and fingers and the base of the hand slipping into the recesses as they would into a worn favourite leather glove. The late afternoon light was wintry and thin and the clouds ragged as they hurried like horsemen across the prairie sky. Raindrops pattered lightly on to my cape. The soft whispering hiss of the wind over the wet and glistening rock and through the short spiky whiskers of coarse grass made starker the emptiness of this almost treeless tract of prairie. About this low scab of rock there was a sense of mystery. In history's dawn the early tenants of the middle flatlands of America used it as their slate and also, perhaps, as a place for their rites. Now it is a puzzle for men to ponder, an enigmatic note cast up on a shore and left by the tide; faded, rainwashed and tantalizing.

There are almost two thousand carvings, petroglyphs as they are more grandly called, on these rock slabs in Cottonwood County in south-western Minnesota, a few miles out of the small town of Jeffers. At first the marks are difficult to discern. You may walk over the quartzite and see nothing, save the scratches ploughed by the glaciers, and the water ripples imprinted in the rock in the age when it was the bed of a great sea. But, as you stare, the rock slowly yields its messages, seeming shyly to unveil its pictures; faintly, and then clearly, like photographic prints emerging in the developing dish; and the eye, growing accustomed, begins to spy dozens when it saw none before. Some are spidery marks, others bold etchings. All are displayed there, innocent and simple, in the manner of pictures pinned up in a primary school for parents' day.

The early Americans depicted the animals with whom they shared these marvellous, vast and undulating plains: rabbits, wolves and lake turtles, and the herds of stately elk and burly bison which they followed in drifting rhythm as the animals munched at the waving grass and mooched on. They depicted themselves, too: matchstick men brandishing spears and clutching atlatls, the catapult devices they used for hurling darts and spears. They drew their chiefs and magicians wearing bison horn helmets; and the prickly pear cactus they used for food and medicine. They worried at the rock to pick out their simple triangular symbol for the thunderbird, a constant and powerful motif in their art, legends and beliefs. To them a thunderstorm was a mighty, dark and frightening eagle-like bird which clutched daggers of lightning in its claws and sometimes threw them to earth in awful anger.

Men began making script on these rocks about three thousand years before the birth of Christ and made their last marks about the middle of the eighteenth century. The last figures they cut were of the horses they adored and which had revolutionized their lives. The Spanish conquistadore Francisco Coronado had brought horses to the Americas early in the sixteenth century and, through inter-tribal trade, and theft and warfare, the use and knowledge of horses crept steadily across the interior.

For the people of the prairie lands the horse was truly a gift from the gods. For perhaps fifteen or twenty thousand years they had been foot nomads; ever since the ancestors of all the aboriginal people of the Americas had entered the continent, presumably from Siberia by way of the Bering Strait ice bridge. They had farmed in a simple way and had stalked the bison, sometimes wriggling towards them with wolf-skins on their backs for disguise. Or they had driven them over ravines to kill them, gorging themselves at once on slippery warm livers and taking the flesh to dry, and the skins for their clothing, their tipis, ropes and thongs, and the bones for tools and weapons.

With the coming of the horse their lives were transformed. They moved out of the dog age, in which dogs were their only servant-beasts, into the horse age. It was one of history's great embracings. Indians and horses fitted together like beautifully machined nuts and bolts. Emancipated now, exulting in splendid and exhilarating mobility, they entered their brilliant and dramatic golden epoch. Freed from hunting on foot, fast and clever on their horses, whooping and vigorous and proud, they were the centaurs of America, the lords of the plains. They hunted with speed. No longer men in wolves' clothing they rode alongside the fleeing hurtling buffalo to bring them down with arrows and lances.

They prized all their horses, and especially the ones the Spaniards had called pintos, or painted horses: the brown and white skewbalds and the black and white piebalds, often with eyes of startling blue, always bright and prancing and muscular.

For the colour, drama and romance of their way of living, and for their horsemanship, the free-ranging mounted men became symbolic in European eyes of all Indians. Other tribes and nations lived, dressed, spoke and fed differently, and won their food and clothing by different means: the immense variety of Indian peoples meant that there could be no such being as a typical Indian. Nor is there now. Yet stories, novels, newspapers and Hollywood presented the plains Indian as the representative. The copper-skinned brave, hawk-eyed, eagle-nosed, straight as a lodge-pole pine astride his war pony, his feathered bonnet flowing thicker than porcupine quills down his back, became the quintessential red man. His very name, Red Cloud, Kills-in-Water, Brown Bear, each a story in itself, seemed the tinder of adventure.

But the horse age had a cruel twist to its glory. Its incandescence was tragically brief. Before many years had passed it was blighted. For the horse was brought to the Indians by white men who in the end were to wipe the red man from the plains, horses and all.

About sixty-five miles south-west of the petroglyphs, near the town of Luverne, is another ridge of the hard rock known as Sioux quartzite. It is called the Blue Mounds. From here, although it is only a low rumple in the sweep of the prairie, you can see between a thousand and two thousand square miles of the plains. It was an important place for the Indians who used to roam the plains as Bedouin do the desert. Among the rocks, where flowers, ferns and cacti grew, in shallow dells where burr oak, wild plum, chokecherry and cottonwood found and provided shelter, they made winter camp. They stalked the buffalo which wandered here; and best of all they waited until the wind blew from the south-east. They knew that buffalo always faced the wind when they fed, and in that place the buffalo would nose and nibble to the edge of the cliff so that it was easy for the men, whooping and waving, to drive them over to their deaths. The first white men here found a huge ossuary, piles of bleached bones beneath the cliffs.

There is something else: from the top of the Blue Mounds to the edge of a ridge there runs a long straight stone wall, one thousand two hundred and fifty feet long, and directly below it are two stone circles. Twice a year, at the spring and autumn equinoxes, you may stand at the upper end of the stone fence and look down it as if sighting down a rifle barrel, and know that the sun will rise directly above the end of the wall; in the same way that you know that only on midsummer's morning will the sun rise directly above the Heel Stone of Stonehenge, built four thousand years ago. Why prehistoric people built the arrow-straight fence at the Blue Mounds no one knows. It lies precisely east and west and perhaps it was used as a navigation marker, as were the intriguing standing stones erected by early travellers in Britain. Like the petroglyphs, like other pieces of the flotsam of time, it stirs imagination. And it is perhaps not too fanciful to speculate that on one equinoctial morning, years ago but not really so long ago, men shivered in the almost-dawn and squinted down their sighting-tube of a wall to see the sun pierce the dark sky; and saw, on the horizon, the first faint dust-smudge of the newcomers from the east, their shadows long on the prairie.

3

A DISTANT THUNDER

Oh give me a home where the buffalo roam.
Dr Brewster Higley

Standing Eagle, his face as brown and wrinkled as a good conker, was making a tipi. Squatting cross-legged, he worked like a wooden-walls sailmaker, his strong leathery big-knuckled fingers looping small, patiently-tied stitches as he sewed pale grey chamois-soft buffalo hides together with sinew. He thought it would take him about a year and a half to complete the task. The making of a real buffalo-hide tipi today is a rare event. The people who know how to make one in the traditional fashion are few, and dwindling.

The tipi is simple and functional and it was the perfect home for the nomadic life on the great plains. The Indians used to say that a beautiful tipi was like a mother, hugging her children to her, protecting them from the extremes of heat and cold. The tipi — the Sioux word means dwelling — is not a wigwam. A wigwam was a shelter of bark and branches and rushes and suited Indians whose lives were relatively settled. The plains Indians, drifting in the slow currents of the woods and prairies, needed a fairly light construction which could be dismantled and re-erected with ease, which would withstand the robust prairie wind, which would be cool in scorching summer and warm in bitter mid-west winters. The tipi was part of the plains Indians' brief horse age, part of the new mobile life. The Indians developed the perfect tipi, a beautiful construction whose shape made it possible to be comfortable inside and to be able to have a fire without the smoke stinging the eyes. In section the tipi was egg-shaped and its frame was not truly conical. It started off as a tripod and against this main frame about twenty long poles were rested and tied. Indians travelled many miles in search of suitable trees for their poles. The best were made from the slender pine they called lodge-pole pine. It had few lower branches and so left few knots when trimmed. The women smoothed the poles with bone. They also tanned and cleaned the skins for the cover and sewed them. The tipi entrance traditionally faced the east and the new day; and this meant that it faced away from the prevailing wind. Also, the cone was tilted so that the weather side was slightly straighter and the poles on the lee side had a greater slant and were more effective buttressing against the wind. The asymmetrical form meant that the smoke-hole, on the lee side of the tipi, was precisely above the fire. Smoke flaps, or ears, were controlled by long poles and could be adjusted to the wind direction like a chimney cowl. The effect of air passing over the ears was to create the perfect airflow conditions to draw smoke out of the tipi so that the interior was comfortable. The exterior was often painted to identify its owner and illustrate his exploits.

Standing Eagle was working with industrious rhythm.

'I was taught how to build tipis when I was young. My people were artistic. The craft was handed down and so what I do now joins me to the past. I am old now and many Indian people do not know how tipis are made, so I want to leave one behind. It will show something of the skills and craft of my people. It will show people in the future something of the people we once were in the days when we were part of this land.'

Standing Eagle, an Ojibwa Indian, whose non-Indian name is George Bryan, was born in northern Minnesota in the early years of the twentieth century when the Indian wars had been over for a couple of decades and the plains Indians, subdued and wretched, were having to find paths out of the wreckage of their traditions. He learned to be a carpenter and engineer and eventually went to work at Pipestone in Minnesota. This was a sacred place for Indians because it was a rich source of a fairly soft red stone, pipestone, from which Indians carved the ceremonial pipes that were central to some of their rituals. These decorated calumets, filled with pungent tobacco and herbs, were regarded as links with the spirits in the sky and as blessings on negotiations, and so the place where the pipestone was quarried was revered and known as Fountain of the Pipe.

In his epic Song of Hiawatha, Longfellow wrote of the great red pipestone quarry:

> And in silence all the warriors
> Broke the red stone of the quarry,
> Smoothed and formed it into Peace-Pipes,
> Broke the long reeds by the river,
> Decked them with their brightest feathers,
> And departed each one homeward...

Today the quarrying of pipestone is reserved by treaty for Indians. They make pipes which are sold at the visitor centre near the quarries. Standing Eagle is one of the best pipemakers and showed me how he cut the stone for the pipe bowl and drilled out the bowl with flint. He smoothed it and polished it with beeswax and it was ready for its long wooden stem. He gave me a cube of pipestone, for luck, and went back to stitching his tipi.

It took him about four years to collect enough skins for it. He was born after the end of the buffalo age, after the end of the most concentrated and largest mass animal slaughter in history, so that even when he was a boy a genuine hide tipi was rare and tipis were mostly made from canvas supplied by the government: where once Indians hunted for their homes, they now queued for them.

Buffalo Bill and marksmen like him hunted the American bison to within a whisker of extinction. At the beginning of the nineteenth century the mightly herds were thick as bees and counted in multi-millions. In 1830 there were said to be more than seventy million of them on the plains, and when pursued by hunters, they thundered in vast masses, making the ground tremble.

The buffalo was a total resource for the plains Indians. It was commissary, armoury and sports store, and Indians gave prayers of thanks over its stripped bones. Its skin made tipis and clothing, its meat was cooked fresh or dried for leaner times, its stomach made a cooking pot, its bladder a water bucket, its brains a tanning paste, its dung a fuel, its ribs sledge runners, its sinews thread, its neck-skin a shield, the rough part of its tongue a comb, its bones an array of knives, scrapers, dice, brushes, needles, clubs, tools and weapons, its tail a fly-swat, its skull an altar, its hair a ball for games.

Indians began to kill more buffalo than they needed for themselves to trade for guns and knives and liquor. But at mid-century there were still fifty million of the animals roaming. The end, though, was not far off. The quickly spreading settlers, the advancing railroad companies, the army and large numbers of sportsmen saw to it that the buffalo were wiped from the plains.

The settlers regarded the buffalo as a pest, an obstacle to land taming. The railroad men sent out hunters to bring in buffalo tongues ('an exquisite dainty', Charles Dickens thought when he was served one in 1842) and steaks for their navvies: William Cody, the most famous of a number of Buffalo Bills, earned his sobriquet as a hunter for the Kansas Pacific railroad. Other hunters went after the hides, especially after the introduction of a process which made large-scale tanning a cheap and profitable undertaking. The plains were littered with hundreds of thousands of skinned carcasses. And, all the time, sportsmen were making excursions into the plains to blast away, leaving the corpses to rot. It was easier than shooting rats in a barrel, and the sportsmen themselves began to complain of the smell of the mouldering bodies.

For the Indians it was like seeing their own blood drip unstaunched into the earth. The army knew it and encouraged the extermination. Fighting Indians with soldiers and carbines was ineffective compared with relentless reduction of their food supply. The Indian wars commander, General Philip Sheridan, well knew the importance of this kind of warfare. In the Civil War he had so laid waste the Shenandoah Valley, the granary of the South, that 'a crow would have had to carry its rations across the Valley.' And of the struggle with the Indians he said that the buffalo hunters had done more in two years to settle the Indian question than the entire regular army in thirty. 'They [the hunters] are destroying the Indians' commissary. Send them powder and lead and let them kill, skin and sell until they have exterminated the buffalo.' The hunter, he suggested, was the forerunner of civilization on the prairies.

The sheer scale of the slaughter was barely credible. The Indians were astonished that the sacred source of so much of importance in their existence had been so brutally and swiftly stopped. In the last days of the buffalo a few Indians grubbed among the dried bones on the prairie, gathering them up to sell for a few cents to button factories or to be ground into fertilizer for white farmers. There was a story that in one place on the prairie a man could walk for a mile on the bones of buffalo.

By the mid 1880s there was hardly a buffalo left. Men sang around their camp fires about the hunting:

'...Tell others not to go, for God's forsaken the buffalo range, and the damned old buffalo.'

The thunder had gone and, for the Indians, a melancholy silence fell over the plains.

The National Museum in Washington noted the silence too, and started a search in 1886. It wanted six buffalo to stuff and put on display because it recognized that probably the creature would soon be as dead as the dodo that sailors had eaten out of existence in Mauritius. It sent a taxidermist to comb the old buffalo lands. Astonishing: in a few years of wantonness the buffalo had melted like snow before the sun, and there was doubt that there would be enough left to put in a glass case. The taxidermist, William Hornaday, heard that in all of North and South Dakota there were only a handful of buffalo surviving.

Not enough for a tipi.

A few more were found in Canada; and a few more here and there. The estimates of the number of buffalo left ranged from thirty-nine to about five hundred. Hornaday and others founded the American Bison Society in 1905 and demanded protection for the beasts. With the help of the New York Zoological Society, and fifteen thousand dollars of government money, a buffalo range was set up in the Wichita National Forest, Oklahoma. In 1907, fifteen buffalo were sent by rail from New York Zoo to Oklahoma. There was huge excitement when the train steamed into the town of Cache. Out here, where the buffalo had roamed the range, a lot of people had never even seen one.

The herd grew over the years to a thousand head and today

there are about fifty thousand head in the United States, all descended from that handful. Many of them are on the open range because a growing demand for their meat makes the raising of buffalo a good and expanding business. In some circles a buffalo steak or buffalo burger is a rather smart thing to order, and restaurants throughout the country have their supplies flown in daily.

Roy Houck, a buffalo rancher for twenty years, has three thousand five hundred head on his fifty thousand acre Triple-U ranch in South Dakota. He gave me lunch of buffalo casserole — 'It's just an old round-up stew' — and asked me how I liked it. I said I liked it a lot. Buffalo has a distinctive flavour, reminiscent to my palate of venison.

Mr Houck fitted my preconception of a prairie rancher. He was weathered and laconic and tough, with sharp eyes that were used to looking at distant horizons. Though more than seventy he was fit and hardworking and made it plain that his guiding principles were the old frontier ones of fierce independence and hard work, jaw set firm against elements and bureaucrats.

At lunch he told how he had developed ranch and herd and a market for his meat. 'All built up by our own efforts with private money. We do not accept any government help — '

'Right on, right on,' a neighbour broke in, approvingly.

'We got our land through hard work,' Mr Houck said. 'It just goes to show that there's opportunity in this world if you're willing to work for it.'

He took me in his pick-up truck to see the herd grazing. We bumped over the prairie beneath a brilliant blue sky until we saw, in the distance, the dark brown smudge of the herd. He said it was worth two and a half million dollars and the calves would sell for five hundred dollars apiece.

'We're fortunate that buffalo are still with us. We owe a lot to those conservationists who saved them seventy years ago. It's wonderful to watch them moving across the range as they did for centuries. Course, raising buffalo doesn't suit everybody. Some folks forget that buffalo are wild animals. They're independent with a strong sense of survival. And they're big. They get to six feet high and two thousand pounds. So you have to have strong fences. And they can't be tamed. I tried to

52

halter-train a little calf for six weeks and she never let up kicking me. And I've never heard of anyone who tried to get buffalo milk.

'You need more land for buffalo, too, much more than you need for cattle. But there are advantages. Buffalo are disease-resistant and you don't have to prepare feed all summer to feed them all winter. They'll forage the year round and dig in the snow with their hooves, so there's a saving on labour and on feeds. They live longer than cattle, thirty years or more, and they reproduce for longer too.'

Nostalgia, Mr Houck thought, played its part in the satisfaction of buffalo raising. And in the eating of them, too. I saw that a meat packer in South Dakota was running an advertisement saying: 'Step back a century — feast on buffalo meat! The buffalo — once slaughtered to near extinction — is back. You can impress your friends and customers with meat that's superior in taste.'

Sure, Mr Houck said, people like to feel they are eating a frontier meal, just as their grandfathers and great-grandfathers did in the old west.

The pick-up truck lurched to a halt and I got off and walked to inspect the herd more closely. The buffalo looked up from their grazing and considered me for half a minute. Then, quite suddenly, as if at a signal, they wheeled and thundered off, their hooves drumming enough to make a mark on a Richter scale. The ground shivered.

The buffalo are only a remnant, it's true, but the sound they make is still loud, exciting and evocative, and we are lucky we can still hear it when we so nearly lost it, the echo of another time.

4
MONUMENTAL MASON

The Indian — Late Terror of the Plains Camped in
Peace with the Conquering Foe.
Buffalo Bill's Wild West Show poster.

Well, no, Mrs Ziolkowski said, her husband was not at home.
At which moment there was a crack and a roar and a rumble on
the mountainside and tons of dynamited dislodged rock
tumbled down. As you can see, she said, he's tied up at the
moment.

Actually, Korczak Ziolkowski has been tied up for more
than thirty years. He is carving the largest statue in the world,
and it is the great work and passion of his life and a matter of
some wonder for the thousands of people who stop to gaze at
his monumental labour. Mr Ziolkowski is not chiselling chips
from a block or marble. With the aid of excavators and
dynamite he is shaping a mountain into a statue of an Indian
chief more than five hundred and sixty feet in height, which is
somewhat higher than St Paul's. It seems it takes a man with a
hard name to do hard things.

In his grappling with the granite Mr Ziolkowski has broken
ribs and legs and damaged his back and suffered two heart
attacks. But he is tough and determined. You can buy pictures
of him to send to your friends and these show a smiling and
weathered shiny-cheeked face with a long bushy Father Christmas beard and a crumpled mountain-man hat, out of the brim
of which someone seems to have taken a bite: perhaps Mr
Ziolkowski, feeling peckish. Anyway, you can see that he is
tough and determined.

Tough? rosy Mrs Ziolkowski echoed with a smile. Tough is not the word.

She told his story with wifely pride. Mr Ziolkowski did the punctuation with his bangs of dynamite. Bruised and chipped, he was nearly seventy years old when I went to inspect his work and was battering away at an arm more than two hundred and sixty feet in length which is to be rounded off with a finger tip about three feet long. He presses on with ferocious energy and hopes to chisel and polish the last details of the statue himself. But, should death or infirmity prevent that, two of his sons, his workmates, will carry on, following his plans and his working model. Mr Ziolkowski made a promise to Chief Standing Bear that the statue would, some day, be finished; and the promise is unbreakable.

Henry Standing Bear was a nephew of Crazy Horse, the Sioux chief who defeated Custer and two hundred and fifty men of the United States Seventh Cavalry at the battle of the Little Bighorn river in Montana in 1876. Crazy Horse was cast by the fates in an heroic and tragic mould, a bright blazing defiant flame which roared up just before his people's fire was extinguished. He was born, in about 1842, at Rapid Creek, Dakota, just as the golden age of the plains Indians was entering its decline; so that in his nostrils was the sniff of a great freedom, and in his mind the stories of that freedom passed down the generations. In the story of the far west his life was a chapter of defiance. He was a warrior and a leader and so his destruction was earnestly and urgently sought by the United States army which knew him, and respected him, as a dangerous foe. Crazy Horse was not one for the council chamber. Not for him the treaty negotiations with the double-dealing cynical arm-twisters who represented the American people in parleys with Indians. Crazy Horse picked up his people's broken banner. He was brave and clever and a shrewd strategist. He was a proud man who championed his people's way of life. Although he must have known that the years of this way of life were numbered, he was uncompromising in his opposition to white encroachment of Sioux homelands. He was the perfect man-of-action counterpart to his great contemporary, Sitting Bull, who was more politician and planner but who, like Crazy Horse, was a determined preacher and leader of resistance.

Under these two, Crazy Horse of the Oglala branch of the tribe, and Sitting Bull of the Hunkpapa branch, the Sioux made their last stand.

Crazy Horse came to prominence when, at the end of the Civil War, the government could afford to bring fuller attention to the west and could now send more soldiers to coerce the Indians who stood in the way of the complete settlement of the plains. Settlers and railroad builders wanted protection. Meanwhile the Indians considered the lies and cheating of the Indian bureau and the War Department, the debris of broken treaties, and sensed that the white men had in mind a final solution to the Indian problem: the expropriation of their lands and a mixture of imprisonment and extermination. For the United States army there began three decades of dishonour and crime and muddle as the bluecoats, many of them ill-trained and ill-equipped both militarily and mentally, brought the red men to heel.

A force of eighty-one soldiers was wiped out in Kansas in 1866 by Sioux led by Crazy Horse. And after that Crazy Horse headed attacks on the railroad builders and never lost a battle. But the railroads were to help strangle the Indians: they split the herds of buffalo on which the Indians depended and made it easier for the hunters who sought meat for the railroad men. The hunters also wanted the hides to sell, and were under orders to kill as many buffalo as possible to encourage the Indians to surrender and enter reservations as paupered dependants of the government.

The invasion of the Black Hills was the turning-point. The Black Hills of Dakota, black when seen from the distance, are a region of dense pine forests about one hundred miles long and fifty miles wide in the west of South Dakota. For the Sioux, who knew them as Pahasapa, they were not only a good place to live and to hunt but they also had a religious significance. And their use of the region was confirmed by the Treaty of Laramie, 1868, under which the Black Hills were made over to the Sioux as a tribal homeland in exchange for their hunting grounds in Kansas and Nebraska. The treaty said that 'as long as rivers run and grass grows and trees bear leaves, Pahasapa the Black Hills, will forever be the sacred land of the Indians.'

Six years after the treaty the megalomaniac Lieutenant-

Colonel George Custer entered the Black Hills at the head of a force of soldiers and gold-hunters. For some time the white men had known that there was gold in the hills and they had been seeping in inexorably, as water into a dry sponge. When Custer's expedition confirmed that the Black Hills were magnificently auriferous the pressure on the region grew as white men trespassed. Crazy Horse urged and led resistance to the invasion of sacred land guaranteed by solemn treaty. The prospectors said to hell with the treaty and demanded free entry — and soldiers to protect them from the Indians.

The Indian Bureau tried to persuade the Indians to sell the Black Hills for six million dollars, the nineteenth-century version of a handful of beads. The Indians refused and the government turned crook again and ordered the Indians on to reservations. The ultimatum to the Indians was impossible for many of them to meet because it ordered them to travel long distances in the bitterness of mid-winter. In the face of this more people joined the movement of defiance under Sitting Bull and Crazy Horse. The government had its excuse for a declaration of war on the Indians and the army was sent to pacify them, a word which today has the ring of a Vietnam war euphemism. The defiant Sioux, with a few allies, formed a mobile force of about two thousand five hundred warriors, and these, the last free red men of the plains, took to the lovely hills of Montana and awaited the advancing soldiers.

Custer, known to white Americans as a colourful, dashing figure, boy wonder of the Civil War, was known to Indians as Long Hair the Squaw Killer for his slaughter of women and children at an Indian camp. As he hurried up the Rosebud river to do battle he was anxious for glory: he had fouled his nest by accusing a member of President Grant's family of corruption, but offered only gossip in testimony, and had been stripped of command on the orders of the enraged President. Now, only because friends had pleaded for him, he was at the head of his troops, certain that the cavalry would sweep the Sioux like a yard broom. He had divided his force into three and was leading one section when, on this Sunday afternoon, Crazy Horse's men fell upon Custer's like a hornet swarm and finished them off in an hour's hot fighting. The Indians cut off the trigger fingers of some and made the little bones into a necklace. Only a cavalry horse survived the battle, and it is now stuffed in a museum. Custer's dash had been a flashy stroke, and his decision to trisect his force a foolish one. But there: he had been bottom of his class at West Point military academy.

In its report of the battle at Little Bighorn the *Bismarck Tribune* wrote that Custer's two brothers, his brother-in-law and a nephew 'who insisted on accompanying the expedition for pleasure' lay close to Custer. The account noted that the 'heads and privates' of some of the dead had been cut off, but the body of the *Tribune*'s own correspondent 'alone remained unstripped and was not multilated.' Perhaps, the newspaper reflected, the Indians had 'learned to respect this humble shover of the lead pencil.' The correspondent's last message to the paper had been: 'By the time this reaches you we will have met and fought the red devils, with what result remains to be seen. I go with Custer and will be at the death.'

America was astounded by the news of the Seventh Cavalry's annihilation; and humiliated too. It was the year of the centennial and the flowering nation was being celebrated. The public demanded the crushing of the Indians.

In its headlines the *Bismarck Tribune* asked: 'What Will Congress Do About It. Shall This Be The Beginning Of The End?'

Whatever the newspaper meant by that final shriek, the battle at the Little Bighorn was indeed the beginning of the end for the plains Indians, a bittersweet victory that presaged defeat. The army moved in in force and the dwindling band of Indians was no match for its firepower. Within months of Little Bighorn the Sioux were treading the shadows of their pursuers. Sitting Bull and some of his tribe fled to Canada in February of 1877 and Crazy Horse, after a debilitating winter on the run, surrendered with hundreds of his men. 'One of the great soldiers of his day and generation,' an army officer said of him. Crazy Horse had no wish to endure the humiliation of reservation life, living on the handouts of the government, and the army arrested and imprisoned him. In September, fifteen months after his whooping triumph over Custer, Crazy Horse was bayoneted to death by a soldier. The official reason given was that he was trying to escape.

There were only some loose ends now. The brave remnants

of Nez Perce Indians were driven out of Idaho and into Montana, and after pursuit, were forced to surrender. In the southwest Geronimo's proudly independent Apaches were subdued, and Geronimo himself, exhibited as a tourist attraction at the St Louis Fair of 1903, died in 1909. Sitting Bull had entered show business for a while as a performer in Buffalo Bill's Wild West Show, but in 1890 was placed under arrest in case he should organize demonstrations or resistance. This dignified old man met the same end as Crazy Horse: he was shot in the back by a policeman, and the authorities were thus rid of what they considered a source of trouble.

The authorities were particularly jumpy at this time because plains Indians were caught up in the fervour of the ghost dance cult. A mystic had prophesied that if tribes danced themselves into trances the earth would be transformed: the buffalo would return, the whites would vanish and the Indians would once more be lords of the plains. It was said that ghost dance shirts would be bullet-proof...and some of the dancers had visions of the new golden age. The ghost dance was harmless; it was a way in which a broken people ameliorated their despair and mourned for themselves. But whites saw it as a resistance movement.

The Seventh Cavalry, who had taken the puerile motto Remember Custer, had their shabby vengeance in the end. About two weeks after the killing of Sitting Bull a group of Sioux were rounded up by the cavalry at Wounded Knee creek in South Dakota. There were about four hundred Indian men, women and children, and about two and a half thousand soldiers. The morning after their surrender the Sioux were being disarmed when a shot was heard. Whether it was deliberately or accidentally fired no one knows. But the jumpy, ill-disciplined soldiers swung their new machine-guns on to the Indians and steadily mowed them down. In their savagery they also cut down some of their own men. A few days later the frozen stiff corpses of the Indians were thrown into a mass grave while the soldiers in their greatcoats and fur caps leant on their shovels and rifles and posed for a gruesome team photograph beside their handiwork. It was a good day for the photograph because the sun was shining brightly.

Wounded Knee was the grave of any remnant of Indian

hopes and the end of the struggle on the great plains. The Indians began to eke out forlorn existences in the reservations. The missionaries swooped in among them and families were broken up as children were sent away to boarding schools to be civilized with the aid of schoolmasters' canes. The white men continued to take their land, by trickery and treaty, and the Indians, robbed, desperately poor, broken and apparently without hope, faded out of sight and out of the minds of the white men and became, quite soon, the forgotten people.

Henry Standing Bear reflected on all these events, on the vivid and defiant life of his uncle, Crazy Horse. From 1927 to 1941 he watched the sculpting of the giant faces of four presidents, Washington, Jefferson, Lincoln and Theodore Roosevelt, at Mount Rushmore in the Black Hills. These heads, carved out of the granite, are sixty feet from chin to top, with noses twenty feet long and mouths eighteen feet wide. More than four hundred and fifty thousand tons of rock were blasted by dynamite from the mountain. Henry Standing Bear was impressed and went to see Mr Ziolkowski with an idea. As he put it, in 1939, there was a need for a great memorial to a great man and his people. After all, the statues of the white men's leaders and generals dotted the land. The Indians were defeated now, reduced and often wretched, but they had once been lords of the plains and forests and were part of the American experience. A noble statue, he said, would serve as a reminder of past glory and as an inspiration in Indians' modern battle for justice and the recovery of dignity and identity.

Henry Standing Bear had come to the right man. Mr Ziolkowski has great imagination and optimism. Moreover, he had worked with the sculptor Gutzon Borglum on the Mount Rushmore project, so he knew a lot about the rare art of megasculpture.

The proposition fired Mr Ziolkowski. There could be no fee for the Crazy Horse monument, but the sculptor reckoned he could make his work pay. He gave up his career as an orthodox sculptor and looked around for a likely mountain. He bought Thunderhead Mountain, near the small town of Custer, and only twenty-two miles from the Mount Rushmore faces, and started work in 1948. The first dynamite charge was fired by

Henry Standing Bear. Mr Ziolkowski did not have much money, less than two hundred dollars, but he started building. He built a log house, started a sawmill and a farm and built up a family of five sons and five daughters. He built a wooden stairway of seven hundred and forty-one steps up the mountain and carried all his materials and tools on his broad shoulders. In the winter, when it is not possible to work on the mountain, he maintains his farm and has developed his home into a large museum and visitor centre. That is how he makes his money and finances his sculpture; he charges tourists who come to his mountain to watch him work, and he sells postcards and souvenirs. On display is his working model of the Crazy Horse statue, brilliant white, twenty-one feet high and weighing sixteen tons. It depicts Crazy Horse in heroic pose, astride a war pony with left arm outstretched, pointing eastwards over the Black Hills.

It recalls the taunt a soldier made when Crazy Horse was captured.

'Where are your lands now?'

Crazy Horse pointed to the Black Hills.

'My lands are where my dead are buried.'

When the statue is completed there will be room on the outstretched arm for four thousand people to stand and a house could be lodged in the nostril of the war pony. The enterprise is a natural source of these eccentric statistics. But one is tempted to say *if* the statue is completed. For the work is awesome. When I stood on a sunny day and watched Mr Ziolkowski's bulldozer, a distant dot like a ladybird, crawling over the mountain, only the crudest outline of the statue could be seen. So far more than six million tons of rock have been removed and there is still a long way to go. It is easy enough to be carried along by the romance of the project, and the Ziolkowskis' enthusiasm. Mrs Ziolkowski, whose life it has been as well, radiates confidence: there is no doubt in her mind that one day there will be a Crazy Horse statue that will truly be a wonder of the world.

And many people are rooting for Mr Ziolkowski, willing him to succeed. They like his independence. He has twice refused government aid for the project and people send along money to aid the work. They write to him, too. One admirer simply addressed his letter to: The Crazy Pole Carving the Mountain.

But his work and vision also touches a vein of prejudice among people who still have a frontier view of Indians. There is still a strain of dislike and suspicion of Indians in South Dakota. Vandals have defaced his sculptures, including his bust of Paderewski, which won first prize at New York World's Fair in 1939; and he is still a target for sneers of 'Indian Lover.'

Mrs Ziolkowski says he finds that sort of thing painful. 'He wants the statue to be, not just for Indians, but for all Americans, a reminder that history has many sides to it.'

There are critics who say that the project is defacing the mountain, and others who maintain that, since Crazy Horse himself would never allow himself to be photographed, it is wrong to attempt a statue of him since there is no authenticated photograph of him among half a dozen likenesses which purport to be of him. The statue, however, is symbolic. And Mr Ziolkowski, who has cut his own burial vault in the rock, goes on doggedly blasting away with his dynamite and drills, making his mountain into an astonishing memorial to the first Americans, what he calls the monument the Indians deserve.

5
RESERVATION STREET

No man should part with his own individuality and
become that of another.
William Ellery Channing

The bar, like many of its kind, was plain and unappetizing.
There was a long counter and behind it a mirror against which
stood a rank of whiskey bottles and glasses. The bartender, in a
long white apron, was neither pleasant nor unpleasant. Most
of the floor was occupied by pool tables with faded baize.
Smoke drifted in the blocks of light over the tables as men
pushed back their hat brims and bent over their cues. There
was a buzz of talk and from the jukebox an occasional country
and western dirge. It was a quiet evening in South Dakota.

'Jesus, that Indian,' a man sitting on a bar stool said,
glancing over his shoulder.

'He gets drunk,' the bartender said, drying a glass.

The Indian was in his early twenties. He poured beer down
his throat in thirsty swallows. On the table beside him was a
pitcher of beer. He was alone, playing pool. He was a little
unsteady on his feet, but his shots were true, his eye and cue co-
ordination being still a step ahead of the beer. His instinct for
the geometry of the game was unerring. He looked like a young
man used to being on his own, used to spending his evenings in
this manner; not blatantly discriminated against, but never
befriended, never said 'hi' to. He was just a lonely Sioux getting drunk.

Until they are thirteen or fourteen many children on reservations are like teenagers anywhere. They smile and laugh and

are curious, open-minded and mischievous. But as they grow older they get an insight into their history and their social and domestic conditions. There dawns a realization of what the future holds: they are at the bottom of the heap and are poorer, less healthy and die younger than their fellow Americans. Their horizons are shrunk by unemployment, poor housing, uncertain education and prejudice. The children see that all around them are people with dignity smashed and hope diminished. Smiles fade, laughter dries. On the threshold of adulthood these young people become apathetic and depressed. They take to drinking and become the cliché: drunken, hapless Indians. In general, Indians have drink problems at a much earlier age than whites. On some reservations more than a quarter of the people are reckoned to be alcoholics. On the Rosebud reservation in South Dakota one-fifth of road crashes cause death, and in three-quarters of accidents people have been drinking. Depending on the area they live in, Indians get into trouble with the law because of drink on a scale twelve to twenty-four times greater than the national average. Drink is the cause of fights, shootings and many road accidents; the murder rate is much higher among Indians than among whites and the suicide rate is more than twice as high. Because of drink many Indians experience bereavement and grief as they grow up, and they drink to dull the pain. On some reservations there is a pervading air of hopelessness, and in these desolate places drinking has almost become a method of suicide.

White men have always been aware of the Indians' vulnerability to drink. Whiskey and other firewater were part of the currency of frontier trade, along with guns, pelts and blankets: a keg of rum could be had for thirty beaver pelts in trading-posts. The liquor offered Indians a swift passage into the states of trance that were valued in their culture. There has been no tradition of ritualized social drinking that is a feature of white society: the aim in Indian drinking, whatever the reason, has always been drunkenness.

Occasionally white people grumble about Indians and drink. 'They get their government money, my money, my tax money, and they spend it all on whiskey and beer,' a man in South Dakota said, when I asked him about Indians. 'They won't work, but we have to keep them.'

But, on the whole, you hear very little of Indians. They are out of sight, under the carpet. Most Americans go through their lives and hardly ever see an Indian in the flesh. There are, after all, about two hundred and fifteen million Americans, and only about seven hundred thousand of them are Indians. They are a remnant.

It would be wrong to suggest that the 'Indian question' — its grim past and unhappy present — troubles the conscience of America. For some Americans, certainly, the condition of the Indian is a source of guilt and shame, a reminder of a wrong done and a duty unfulfilled. But most Americans do not care at all. The 'Indian question' is not something that touches their lives.

What the white man did to Indians during his settlement of America amounts to a hideous catalogue of cruelty. And while it is not my purpose to indulge in restrospective anger, I do not think it possible to understand Indian difficulties and attitudes without knowing something of the events and influences which have shaped them; and Hollywood's history of the west falls somewhat short of an accurate impression.

George Washington wrote that 'the basis of our proceedings with the Indian nations has been and shall be justice.' For the next hundred years the basis of American proceedings with the Indians was injustice; and the extensions of them were rob- bery, fraud, corruption, slavery and genocide.

In early contacts with white men, many Indian tribes were devastated by diseases like mumps, diphtheria and measles. This was an unfortunate side-effect of the meeting of races; though occasionally whites employed germ warfare by giving the clothing of smallpox sufferers to Indians, the quicker to exterminate them in an area they coveted. Meanwhile whole tribes were shifted from one region of the country to another so that their land could be settled. But in the end there was con- quest and its numerous shabby, shaming chapters.

The American republic, which had been a gamble in the eighteenth century, was an enormous adventure in the nine- teenth. The dizzying progress of the new nation filled the hearts of many men. The belief that, somehow, the Almighty was directing it was profound. 'We Americans are the peculiar chosen people, the Israel of our time,' Herman Melville wrote. And a senator said: 'God has marked the American people as His chosen nation to finally lead in the regeneration of the world.' The conquering urge was ennobled by John O'Sullivan, editor of the *Democratic Review*, who wrote of America's 'manifest destiny to overspread the continent allotted by Providence.' The flag went west and in its name men struggled, dug, cut, built. 'Indians' bones must enrich the soil before the plough of civilized man can open it,' a lawyer wrote in 1839. Mild men saw Indians as an inconvenience in the path of civilization; harder ones saw them as vermin. 'I have never in my life seen a good Indian except when I have seen a dead Indian,' James Cavanaugh, a Congressional delegate, said, encapsulating a widely held view at a time when the slaughter of large batches of Indians was applauded by press and people. 'The more we can kill this year, the less will have to be killed next war.' General William Sherman said. 'They all have to be killed or maintained as a species of pauper.'

Morality being to some extent in the eye of the beholder, the nineteenth-century view of the Indian and his place in the scheme of things was different from the modern one. In the governor's reception room in the state capitol building in Pierre, South Dakota, is a huge nineteenth-century painting by Edwin Blashfield which innocently illustrates the old attitude perfectly. Its effect is shocking; and Richard Kniep, the governor of South Dakota, who showed it to me, agreed that many people were embarrassed by it. 'Some wish it were not on show and I must say I don't like the subject myself. But it is part of our history and it has a place.' The picture shows a young woman in heroic pose, the spirit of South Dakota, pushing westwards. Two men with her, a bearded one bearing a gun and representing the army, and the other, clutching a pistol and representing the settlers, are knocking Indians to the ground and trampling over them: it is the march of civilization.

The Indians were not all killed, of course, and once conquered and corralled, they were, in General Sherman's cynical words, maintained as a species of pauper. They moved into their reservation age, a dejected and rotting people, to live on government handouts. They continued to suffer from the diseases that spread in poor conditions; and they suffered, too, at the hands of the government's Indian department, which was riddled with fraudsters and thieves. Meanwhile, in the footsteps of the soldiers and settlers trod the teachers and missionaries. No doubt they had righteousness, perhaps compassion, in their hearts; but to many Indians they must have seemed as carrion crows as they settled on the tribes, sometimes competing for converts, and began obliterating native culture and religion. The massacres stopped at last, but the purloining of Indian lands went on, legalized or otherwise. Between 1887 and 1934, for example, Indians lost more than half their land; and the best land at that. There was a prolonged attempt to get Indians to assimilate, to become neo-white men, but the effort only partly succeeded: the deracinated Indians wanted to be Indians and their views on the way that life should be lived were different from the white man's. It was not easy to teach a man to be a farmer when he said: 'You ask me to plow the ground. Shall I take a knife and tear my mother's breast?'

For forty years or so after the crushing of Indian resistance in 1890, they were an impoverished, virtually forgotten, people. In 1903 a man whose job was to care for Indians was asked by the board of Indian commissioners:

'You told us they were dying off pretty fast?'

'Yes sir, a lot of the older people are.'

'Is there any special cause for that?'

'Nothing; there is no new disease; I do not see anything other than the want of hope.'

In the 1930s, however, after an investigation revealing the extent of government mismanagement of Indian affairs, reforms were instituted which permitted tribes to set up their own governments in their reservations and stopped the continuing loss of tribal land. Indians had been declared American citizens in 1924. Much of the steam ran out of the reform programme eventually, and in the 1950s the government tried a policy of withdrawal from its responsibilities for Indians. It failed, and its legacy was intensified Indian distrust of government policies.

In the 1960s and 1970s Indians began to heat the cinders of hope. Their position was still bad overall, but there had been some improvements. At the end of the Indian wars their population had been a quarter million; seventy years later it was three times that. Their health standard lagged behind that of the general population, but was better. In the 1960s and 1970s their life expectancy improved from forty-four years to sixty-three. Thousands of Indians had been assimilated into white society and more Indians were experiencing full education. As I saw for myself in several parts of the United States not all Indians were at the bottom of the heap: I talked and dined with Indian families enjoying housing and a style of life many Europeans could never aspire to. On a more modest scale I went to reservations where the physical standards were perfectly agreeable.

But the picture is patchy. Indians are, on the whole, the poorest of the poor and many of them live in wretched conditions, their lives damaged by ill-health, bad housing, second-rate education, alcoholism, white prejudice and an unemployment rate around forty per cent. 'Some companies would go broke before they would hire an Indian or a black,' a Minnesota Indian said.

Through demonstrations, lobbying and occasional clashes with authority, and certainly a steady hardening of their attitude, Indians have been making their presence felt more effectively. It is not easy because there is no tradition of Indians acting in concert: as the white man has always known, to his advantage, there is no Indian homogeneity. In outlook, tradition, language, customs, Indian tribes are as disparate as, say, Scots and Sardinians. In recent years, however, Indians have been trying to act together to strengthen their influence. On one thing they certainly agree. The common target for their contempt is the government's Bureau of Indian Affairs which has, during its one hundred and fifty years' history, built a reputation for cheating and incompetence and lying. The Bureau is supposed to protect Indian interests and, especially, their threatened lands. But, in keeping with its tradition, it has been signing agreements on behalf of tribes under which mineral rights are leased outrageously cheaply to private enterprise. For example, at a time when coal was worth about thirteen dollars a ton, the Bureau negotiated a 'chickenfeed lease' which gave a tribe about seventeen cents for the coal mined on its land.

As it happens, the mineral wealth which lies under Indian reservation land may prove to be the springboard in the Indian struggle for justice, much more effective than the sporadic demonstrations and relatively low-key assertion movement of the 1960s and 70s. Indians were pushed on to what was once considered entirely poor land; but recent prospecting has revealed that below the surface of some of it are important deposits of coal, oil, gas, uranium and other minerals. Better led, better educated, a number of tribes are seeking much better deals with mining companies. Suddenly they find themselves energy-rich and sought after. And some Indian leaders believe that hard bargaining and fair prices for minerals represent the Indians' last chance of getting out of the quagmire of poverty.

They do not believe that the Bureau for Indian Affairs will be much help in getting just prices. Although the Bureau is there to improve Indian living conditions, about four-fifths of its budget is swallowed up in its own bureaucracy and it is suffocated by paperwork. Indians tell a joke about the Bureau which I heard several times: 'Just before Custer went to the battle of the Little Bighorn he sent a note to the Bureau saying: "Do nothing till I get back." '

2

As well as fighting for better mineral deals Indians are also increasingly insisting on their timber, water, fishing and hunting rights, sometimes to the annoyance of whites who have been used to treading on Indians rather than paying them dues. They are also getting compensation for some of the swindles of which they have been victims. Their relationships with government, the law and white communities are complex and varied; but the mood among Indians is for greater management of their own lives and a larger say in the shaping of their own destinies and those of their children. The true emancipation of the Indian, however, will be a long time coming: the dealings between paleface and red man have left an enormous Gordian knot.

And meanwhile, for many thousands of Indians, there remains the struggle with loss, poor circumstances and reduced hope. Many move off their reservations to seek better things in the cities, but often do not find them. 'It's hard,' Janice Donnelly, an Ojibwa woman working at the native American centre in Minneapolis, said. 'It's hard to find accomodation and we have big problems with slum landlords exploiting people. It's hard to get a job, hard to escape discrimination.

'This centre is a focus, a meeting place, an advice office, a clinic, a recreation centre, a training school. It's a place where we encourage hope and pick up the pieces. We help alcoholics and we help with education. We encourage kids not to drop out of school and try to help people out of their despair. This part of the city has a lot of Indians, but it's still a white man's world. We try to help people cope with that, and also retain their Indian identity. It is the loss of identity that is at the root of many problems. But I think things are improving slightly. We are getting better educated, learning to play it the white man's way, but understanding more of our own history, how it all happened. More of us are beginning to rediscover a pride in being Indian.'

One night, in St Paul, I was invited to a pow-wow at a school. In a crowded room some men sat in a circle around a drum and beat it with insistent rhythm and sang and chanted. Young men had been out on to the streets and had rounded up a few Indians who were drunk and had brought them in to feed them and sober them. Many of the people there were poor, but as a guest I was, in accordance with custom, given food first. The pow-wow is a regular event. It is an opportunity for people to be together and be themselves, unselfconscious, in what has become to some extent an alien land. It is also a way in which adults pass on what is left of their culture. In that schoolroom there was a huddled and tribal feeling, as if the room were a tipi; and the drumming went on relentlessly.

Some pow-wows are large affairs where Indians dance in native costume, not always authentic, and sometimes for the benefit of tourists and commerce. But many of them are for the Indians themselves, a way of keeping a hold on identity and history. I went to one in a hall where the drums throbbed for two days and the cars outside carried stickers like *Custer Had It Coming*. Bright as popinjays in gaudy feathers and beads hundreds of Indians danced for hours. 'Everybody dance:

inter-tribal!' called an announcer. This pow-wow was no exhibition for white entertainment, but a private ritual and gathering for Indians.

A man said: 'It's so we don't forget who we are.'

6
GOOD EARTH

O beautiful for spacious skies,
For amber waves of grain.
                    Katharine Lee Bates

I grew to appreciate the prairie. Its vastness and quality of being immeasurable was at first disconcerting, but I came to terms with it; and its nakedness and deep stillness provoked, not melancholy, but a sense of freedom in which I lost track of time. It encouraged me to luxuriate in unaccustomed introspection. I tramped over it on bright sharp days, when the sky, a bigger sky than I had ever known, was a radiant blue; and the crisp autumn air, hinting at winter, made me button my coat.

There is not much point in ransacking the lexicon to describe the prairie. It is simply astonishing. It is difficult to paint, for no canvas or artfulness can really show you its daunting size; and few photographs can convey something of its immensity. Its horizon seems beyond reach, and you walk it for hours but seem not to move, as if walking a treadmill. It is like a gently heaving ocean that a magician long ago made rock. James Fenimore Cooper wrote of the prairie being 'not unlike the ocean when its restless waters are heaving heavily.' He tired of the sameness of the landscape; and so too did Charles Dickens who saw it in 1842 and wrote of 'solitude and silence reigning paramount around ... lonely and wild, but oppressive in its brown monotony ... not a scene to be forgotten, but scarcely one to remember with much pleasure.'

The first time I went to the prairie I stayed on a farm in Minnesota. On the way there the Greyhound bus went through Sauk Center where Sinclair Lewis lived and whose mid-west small town life he portrayed in *Main Street*. The farm was typical of the region: the farmer and his wife sprang from Finnish and German stock, they raised corn and cattle and they were devout Christians. The farmhouse had religious mottoes on its walls and the farmer's wife was a Sunday School teacher. When I arrived she said a prayer of thanks for my safe arrival. In and around the house the atmosphere was quiet. The pace of life was steady and rhythmic, unhurried, and the people absorbed themselves in it. They were welcoming and kindly, but employed words sparingly. On Saturday night the family took it in turns to have a sauna bath and afterwards we all sat, pink and beswaddled, silently eating freshly cooked popcorn from large bowls and watched a football match on television. There was not much for me to do on the farm. I helped to squeeze apples in a press to make the apple juice which was drunk at most meals. I was taken to a church service and a bible class. Otherwise I walked for miles over the prairie, enjoying the peace and hugeness of it all.

Perhaps the immensity of the prairie was even more impressive for me because I had spent the previous eight years in Wales which is small, green and mountainous, small enough to be popped into America's waistcoat pocket. Minnesota alone is more than ten times the size of Wales. I reflected, as I walked, on the Welsh people who migrated to the prairie region in the nineteenth century. 'Prairies so flat,' wrote one, 'that it made my eyes ache to look at them.' Another wrote mouth-wateringly to friends and relatives in Wales of 'prairies where the grass grows higher than a cow's belly,' where 'the tax gatherer only calls once a year and then it is only a trifle.' And yet another said bluntly: 'Oh, you unhappy Welshmen, why do you not emigrate to Iowa instead of quarrelling over the lack of land and poverty in the mountains of Wales?'

The road to bliss though was not entirely without obstacles. We hear a lot of the trek westwards, nothing of the eastwards-ho! trudge by the defeated. The prairie can be pitiless. In winter, in the cold that shrivelled their hands and faces and hopes, this must have seemed a God-forsaken region to some of those who emigrated. For them dreams ran rancid in the reality of making a new life on the plains. They exchanged their small hilly country for the flat, endless and hostile prairie, enduring disease, the bitterness of winter, attacks by resentful Indians and the unbearable heat of summer.

Even when I stopped the eccentric activity of walking the prairie, and adopted the normal procedure of driving over it, its flatness and seemingly limitless sweep were just as awesome, the sky and horizon merging into a blue smudge.

The bareness would be almost lunar, except that it is punctuated. Water stores are held aloft on stilts like soccer balls about to be thrown into play. Often, they have the name of the town painted on them. There are shiny cigar tubes of silos, spindly wind pumps and squat conical grain stores. There are new farmhouses built alongside the wooden ones that grandfather built in the days when the prairie was horse-ploughed. And these old unwanted homes now sag, peeling and grey, with sightless windows. Renovated, cared for, they might have lasted for generations; but people had the desire and the cash to build anew, and cast off homes like old blue jeans. A good number of the barns, though, are originals. They are Scandinavian in appearance, huge and often red in colour. By the barns stand plump stacks of yellow corn cobs, and the unharvested corn is a luminous gold against the darkening cobalt of a sunset sky. Where the harvesters have been the corn has been shaved off the land to reveal through the stubble a rich black soil. Along the country roads, the back roads, lie little townships with populations of two or three hundred, or maybe seventy or eighty, an occasional airstrip and multi-function stores and workshops advertising a mixture of wares and talents: Cheese and Antiques, Airplanes and Sewing Machines Sales and Service.

And there is the occasional wry sign: *Give Thanks — Take a Farmer to Lunch.*

These days there are fewer farmers to take to lunch. The agricultural life has become agri-business, mechanized, computerized, chemicalized, financierized. The age of the small-time farmer in his little house on the prairie, a key figure in American growth, is over. At the beginning of this century a third of Americans lived on farms; so that if the land is today not strong in the actual experience of many Americans, it is certainly strong in their family backgrounds and emotions. Today, however, only one American in thirty lives on a farm, and about seven-tenths of people registered as farmers are not full-time farmers at all, but have to supplement their incomes by working as plumbers, engineers, office workers and salesmen. The trend in American agriculture is to large and highly mechanized farms, highly capitalized and exploited to every last square inch of land. The modern super-farmer is the other side of the moon to the hayseed of popular fiction: he is a bit of a financier, and adept market forecaster, a man at home with complex machines and computer read-outs. And he is efficient. An American farmer feeds fifty-nine people, three times the number of people fed by one farmer in western Europe.

Prairie soil gives them a head-start. A settler wrote home to his family in 1856: 'I am sure there is no more fertile land in creation than in the state of Iowa… after ploughing it once it is like a garden and they can raise anything on it. If this were populated by good men it would be a second Canaan.'

But a price is exacted for the efficient and intensive farming of this soil. Over-tilling is causing erosion. The topsoil is being blown and washed away. You can see it lying, like soot, along the sides of the roads. In winter it blackens the snow. It is whipped by the wind into dust storms. Farmers know about erosion, but the depth of their credit, the extent of their investment in machines, drive them to farm to the limit, to the edges of the road, and beyond the limits of conservation. They get plenty of warnings that the black soil of the plains is finite, that over-tilling may lead to the creation of another dust bowl of the kind which ruined farmers in the 1930s. But many of them think the fears are exaggerated.

I heard a lot about the argument when I worked on the *Worthington Globe*, the lively and well-produced daily in the town of Worthington, in south-west Minnesota. I met some farmers who were going against the trend and planting hedges and trees to help prevent soil erosion. I also met David Benson, a tall and bearded young farmer, who is being determinedly unfashionable because he has strong views about land use. He has a one hundred and sixty acre farm growing corn, soy, beans, oats and wheat. He raises cattle and sheep — and he still uses horses, something which makes him a prairie oddity.

'For me farming is not a quick cash turnover business as it is for many men. For me it's something for life. Since I was a boy, half the people round here have quit the land and moved into the towns. The trend is to larger farms, and energy-intensive agriculture. In America we are turning petroleum into food and we are very good at it. The determining factor in agriculture is credit: if you can get the money you'll probably be a success. But it's a short term economic gain. It may be only profitable for a hundred years. And that's nothing. After all, only a hundred years ago this land was homesteaded... the Indians were driven off and the raw prairie was put to the plough. But we haven't learned what it means to farm in the long term. We certainly don't have a commitment to soil fertility. We are a wastrel people, exploiting the soil with no eye to the future.

'We over-fertilize and have a problem with surpluses. Around here you can easily raise, say, a hundred bushels of corn an acre. That's within the capability of the soil. But to push it to a hundred and fifty, as many do, you have to put in a vast amount of energy. Farmers are squandering and there is an almost irresistible pressure to do so. We have a crass materialistic view of the land and that is a reflection of our culture. We are much concerned with what we can derive immediately. We are not concerned for our children or our children's children. We have a potential for paradise on earth here. What are we doing? Squandering. It's a social and ecological crime.

'It is only the fortune of the weather that we haven't had more serious erosion. Erosion is slow. You don't see your wealth go down the river in one year, but you see a few per cent going each year. For myself I try to treat the land carefully and farm in a long-term way. I don't use nitrogen fertilizers. I guard against erosion by rotating my crops and ploughing with a chisel plough which does not do so much damage. I grow cover crops in winter, like clover, as you do in England, so that there is something on the land. Not many do that, so we have a vast black desert in the winter stretching from North Dakota to Kansas.

'In other ways I try to be more in tune with the land. I do a lot more work than is usual with my body. I have machinery but it is second-hand. I handle the hay and move the manure without machines, and I have a team of two Percheron horses. I don't envisage a wholesale return to the horse in America: that's just too romantic. But I think there is room for a team on every farm. We mow with them, haul with them and use their manure. They earn their keep and they are renewable because they raise colts. And they are a joy. They're good for the mind. And who can say — with the rising price of oil people may eventually come to see the horse as important again, not a luxury. I'd like to see people embracing some of the old values again, but it's difficult. Modern agriculture destroys rural society, and land is fantastically expensive. I rent this farm from my dad. And with land around here selling at a thousand to two thousand dollars an acre it would be almost impossible for me to buy my own farm. Some people think I'm crazy, with my horses and ideas, but they can see that I work hard and they respect that.'

On a bitter December evening he invited me to join a group of friends and neighbours at supper. For fun we rode across the prairie on a horse-drawn wagon, wrapped in heavy rugs and furs against the biting wind. We crowded into the farmhouse for hot cider and supper. Afterwards everyone sang songs and every adult and every child told a short story, a joke, or recited verse. In the light of the cracking fire and the candles these rosy-faced men, women and children, in heavy wool plaid shirts, looked like a picture that Norman Rockwell might have painted. At last, when it was time to go, we were all given lighted candles with instructions to keep them lit until we reached our homes, so that we should have good luck in the coming year.

Cupping hands to keep the flames alive, we made our various ways, like glow-worms, across the flat starlit prairie.

7

YOUR MONEY OR YOUR MONEY

The whore and gambler, by the state
Licensed, build that nation's fate.
William Blake

No oasis, Las Vegas. Although in the desert, and reached by way of cactus-sentried roads over baked, cracked and inhospitable land, it is the antithesis of haven. Far from being a refuge, a tranquil pool, a staging post and place of refreshing fertility, it is an excrescence. For all its flash and jingle and teeming crowds, its atmosphere is of soulless emptiness and impermanence: its buildings seem like scenery in a Hollywood Western set. Las Vegas is certainly no Xanadu. Its pleasure domes are sprawling and gross, not stately: and it is a city in which there is nothing of elegance. It is highwayman and whore on the desert road, a city both veneer and venereal, dedicated to waste and excess, heartless and without a heart; a town where, probably, nothing good or worthwhile has ever happened, nor ever will.

It is not surprising to learn that Las Vegas started life as a Union Pacific railroad depot in 1905, a tent and shanty dump, because it still has that insubstantial, arid and history-less air about it. Many cities owe their existence and development to entrepreneurial vigour, robust commerce and a measure of greed: so does Las Vegas in its singular way. But, essentially, its development from dusty desert township to money machine is owed to gambling, divorce, the profits of crime, prositution and pornography. It is owed, too, to Howard Hughes who went off his head, to the atom bomb and the hydro-electric

78

power of the Hoover dam. This great white wedge in the canyon is the harness of the awesome might of the Colorado river, and the power it generates is spectacularly and boastfully frittered by the folks at Glitter Gulch.

I was surprised and disappointed by Las Vegas. I think because of what I had read, from the way it was advertised, I had expected to find something more rollicking and more colourful, and more human and more fun. Its publicists call it the entertainment capital of the world, and it promises much; but, even allowing for the adman's preposterous hyperbole, it is a curiously unexciting place, and really rather small and irritating. All the fun of the fair? No, sir. It lacks a breeziness you might expect a resort to have. It is not amiable. It is not carefree — it is depressingly earnest and intense. Entertainment capital simply means there is no bedtime, non-stop play, suspended responsibility, a huge and boggling industry for the relief of lust, a stream of overpaid entertainers (a few of them legendary for their grossness and petulance), the use of a myriad of electric light bulbs and a ceaseless razzly celebration and exploitation of spotlit breast and spangled bum.

I suppose that my credentials for writing about Las Vegas may not be the best: gambling holds no interest for me, and so you might say that my writing about the place is about as useful as asking a eunuch to describe a night passed in a bordello. But I neither approve nor disapprove of gambling, so I grind no axe in that respect. Nothing, though, neither film nor serious television documentary, adequately prepares you for the sheer scale of gambling and the regiments of its leaden, deadened practitioners; nor for the atmosphere of plutolatry and the sense of waste; nor for the relentless grim-faced rigid management of the gaming hangars.

It is a vulgar place in which there are numerous small vulgarities, of which you have heard, but which still make you blink — like the little gingerbread chapels with their pink-neon galilees, and twee names like Hitchin' Post, where you may marry not very seriously; and, later perhaps, unreeve that rope in the easy-divorcerama courthouse. It is an industry: the marriage rate in Nevada is about one hundred and sixty-six per thousand, compared with the national figure of ten per thousand; and the divorce rate runs at seventeen per thousand, compared with the national figure of under five. The Chapel of the Fountain, open eight a.m. to midnight, offered, I noticed, a wedding special for twenty-nine dollars, plus free wedding creed — order of service — toasting-glass, and photograph-frame; Mastercharge and BankAmericard accepted.

Inevitably there are nuptial wheezes thought up by idle people, trying, like Caligula, to salt their jaded palates. There was a wedding in one of the cheap little tinsel chapels where the bride was attended by fourteen bridesmaids who were naked but for red boots and top hats.

No, what Las Vegas lacks is genuine fun and the humour that springs from human warmth. Hot it may be in Nevada, but there is in Las Vegas an eerie bloodless cold: it is a spiritual Baked Alaska. Laughter here is hollow, more the cackle of old dockside bints. The smiles, such as they are, are made merely by muscles and teeth, rarely by eyes and humour and pleasure and contact.

It *is* democratic though, unlike some resorts elsewhere. The modest farmer may stand alongside the tycoon, for there is equality in front of the roulette wheel, just as there is in front of the firing squad: and in both cases the odds are stacked in favour of the management. There is no Jackpot Street in Las Vegas, but there is a Bonanza Road. There is also a Paradise Road, and a sign which says Entering Paradise. I recall saying these two words — 'Entering Paradise' — to myself as, weary after a day's driving and an evening strolling Sodom's boulevards, I slipped gratefully into bed in the hotel — only to emerge at once with a roar as I discovered, uncomfortably, that although the bed was neatly made, with crisp hospital corners, the bedclothes had manifestly not been changed, and that the previous occupant, perhaps a punter from Kalamazoo, ecstatic with jackpot, or disconsolate in loss, and presumably awash with the champagne which Las Vegas has in boasted abundance, had also been incontinent.

2

In the last century people rushed in their thousands to parched and forbidding Nevada to dig for silver and to carry the stuff off. In the second half of the twentieth century people rush in their millions to throw it all back. The leading industries of the Silver State are listed as gambling, tourism, mining, metal processing and the raising of beef cattle and sheep. The Las Vegas area is home for more than half of Nevada's half million people and the state derives half its income from gambling. Thus the people of Las Vegas, like gerbils, have adapted happily to life in their dusty desert valley. They inhabit cavernous halls of gambling where there is no proper time of day; where, indeed, time itself seems to have been suspended, for the gaming houses are clockless. And here they have an amicable working arrangement with the American public: if you will be our compliant victims, they say, we will be delighted to act as temptress, tumbler, fool and cutpurse. The great Comstock silver lode, on which Nevada's early brash growth and statehood were founded, may have petered; but the lode of cupidity on which Las Vegas feeds and grows is as argentiferous as it is bottomless; and every year the gamblers, large and small, fly away rueful and leave behind more than a thousand million jingling silver dollars.

Henry Comstock, who gave his name to the Nevada silver lode which was discovered in 1859, later lost everything — like many other visitors to Nevada since. In due course, looking for something at the end of another rainbow, he grew depressed and blew his brains out. Nevada withered as the silver was worked out and by the 1930s was economically and administratively close to collapse, a state of ghost towns and bleak outlook.

But in 1931 Nevada made gambling legal and the divorce laws easier, so that there began a trade in transients, gamblers and the unhappily married in search of release. The building of the Hoover Dam and the later establishment of a nuclear industry on the vast Nevada proving grounds helped bring prosperity. After the Second World War, Las Vegas, like the bombs, mushroomed. Some of the early growth, the building of hotels and casinos, was financed with the proceeds of criminal rackets, and naturally enough in such a boom town, embezzlement was for a number of years an element in Las Vegas life, the profits of casinos being skimmed and spirited away. The pattern changed as wealthy individuals like Howard Hughes moved in. Corporations began to buy and build, and exhibited their corporate *machismo* by building enormous hotels and gambling halls that would garage zeppelins. Their entertainment centres popped up like forced rhubarb.

Because taxes on gambling are such a large part of the state's income, the gaming agencies enforce strict rules to sluice and draw off the torrents of money. There is a large staff of auditors and investigators constantly analysing and patrolling and peering to detect and discourage those who flutter to Las Vegas as moths to a flame, the greedy, the venal and the ingenious.

It means that there is in Las Vegas a pervading air of suspicion. Everyone who has anything to do with gambling is watched. And the watchers, too, are watched. Las Vegas is a city of spy-holes and beady, swivelling eyes.

Everyone believes that everyone else has fingers like fish hooks. Fun is shallow and the mistrust is deep. The casino operators have originated a whole sub-culture of private laws and rituals to prevent conspiracy and cheating. The dealers and players are observed from behind two-way mirrors, through television cameras, and from hides in which the security men huddle like ornithologists, eyes skinned for the Vegas thieving magpies. If a dealer scratches his nose the action can be recorded on videotape. Dealers must not wear clothing in which the gambling chips could be secreted, their hands must be clearly seen by the observers, and when they reach the end of their shifts and hand over to their reliefs they must hold their palms to the ceiling where watchers in their priestholes may see that they are empty. In some casinos the dealers may not wear long ties because these have in the past been used as receptacles for palmed chips. On the floor of the casino observers pose as customers and strollers and watch from the corners of their eyes for dealers in league with gamblers, for marked cards and shaved dice. And, up in the catwalks and from behind the mirrors, more watchers prowl. No one is left alone to count the takings. When the swag from roulette, dice games, blackjack, baccarat and bingo is counted there are usually three people present — and they in turn are watched through mirrors or television monitors.

The slot machines of Las Vegas, those little money mills, their performances, their jackpots, monitored by computer, are also watched carefully. The dishonest try to beat the machines by drilling holes in them, using discs instead of dollars, or jamming the coin-slots. The ratchety jangling of these machines is part of the insistent noise of Las Vegas. As you walk down The Strip, the main avenue where many of the large hotels and casinos are, you see that there are tens of thousands of them, occupying every available space. They stand, rank upon rank, in hotel lobbies, supermarkets, shops and bars, their handles pulled relentlessly by legions of mostly middle-aged and elderly men and women, who stare grim-faced at the mesmerizing spinning dials. They are the play-things of the American menopause. The players are obsessed: one hand on the lever, the other hand clutching a stack of dollars or quarters, feeding the machines with money, calling out for change rather than leave a machine they believe will soon vomit silver. It is as if the players themselves are mechanical, as if they are controlled by cogs and governors on a production line, and I wondered if they suffered bandit-elbow. There is an awful morbid fascination in observing them, the modern equivalent of pressing noses to a window at Bedlam. And they are at it every hour of the day and night.

Out on The Strip, in the warm air, all is splashy glitter. The sights compete with the sounds. It is an avenue of golden rains and Roman candles, a perennial electric November the Fifth. There are coloured fountains and floodlights, spotlights and flashing signs, some of them quite enormous. One sign is said to use enough electricity in a single day to light five thousand houses: and Las Vegas is like that: the biggest this, the biggest that, ten million this, ten million that, full of tiresome statistics. After walking for a while you wander into one of the hotels, The Dunes, Caesar's Palace, MGM Grand, The Desert, The Sands, The Frontier, The Stardust, and so on; into the conditioned air, past the automaton grannies and plump matrons and their glazed husbands lined up on one-armed bandit duty, whiling away middle age. They do not smile, even when they win. Further in, there is brassy glamour and gloss and carpets thick as moss. The casinos are crowded. There are big, wedge-shaped men in Stetson hats, embroidered shirts and bootlace *bolas* ties held by jewelled turquoise clips. They wear tooled Texan boots and they really do chomp on their cigars, just as you've been told. There are men in smart dark suits and men in loud holiday checks, and, on their arms, their decked-out wives and girlfriends that put you in mind of what Frank Sinatra would call broads. They are poolside-brown and giddy with martini and smile brightly at everything. At a craps game, where people bet on the fall of dice, the dice probably made by the Nevada Dice Company to exacting requirements and used for one day only, a man moans and croons at the dice as they are shaken and rolled:

'Do it for me little babies! Roll for me, babies! Oh, little babies! Come seven, little babies! Make it seven! Oh, shoot!'

At the gaming tables sit the shills, shiny girls with low-cut dresses who flutter their eyelashes and moisten their appliqué smiles: they are paid by the casino to attract gamblers; and they sometimes get tips from gamblers who score a big win. The cocktail waitresses in their bodices and tiny skirts slither through the press of people to dispense free drinks and cigarettes to their serious gamblers, and they, too, can get large tips. Meanwhile the roulette balls stutter and the stakes are raked away like autumn leaves.

For gamblers of another kind, serious men in dinner jackets and women in long dresses, there is the ritual of baccarat, with its eight packs of cards, given an aura of mystery by being played in a hushed and roped-off area, though a game requiring no skill. There is keno, a version of bingo, where the odds in favour of the house are the heaviest of those in all the games; and there are grim games of blackjack beneath the mirrors. Blackjack attracts attention because a highly numerate player with his wits about him and an ability to remember the cards dealt can improve his chances of winning. The dealers' faces are pale and immobile and behind them the boot-faced pit bosses, neat and suspicious, with darting eyes, men who seem to have laughed for the last time twenty years before, watch closely. Some casinos have banned gamblers too good at blackjack; and the local newspapers are full of advertisements for blackjack systems and there are dozens of books available which offer advice. The Howard Grossman Blackjack Academy, for example, offers instruction day and night. Do they really teach blackjack at four in the morning? Most casino operators, apparently, say they regard such card-counting systems as bunk; and probably they are right, though they seem to get upset about gamblers with systems all the same. Gamblers grumble, but who cares about gamblers?

If you tire of the casinos, there are the shows. The revues in Las Vegas hotels are dazzling, gaudy enough to have pleased the emperors of Rome: tableaux of orgies and other exotic scenes; fountains and waterfalls, live camels, horses, elephants and monkeys dressed as Red Indians. And girls, of course: extravagant dishes of naked sequinned chorines, girls in bath-tubs dressed in bubbles, girls in fantastic costumes so glamorous that oglers' cigars get chomped to bits, and girls in pink feathers. The feathers for one show cost nearly eighty thousand pounds. You cannot believe that feathers could cost so much. But there: Las Vegas and its statistics again. Biggest, longest, tallest, fattest, grossest.

3

Cruellest, too.

The perfect showgirl in Las Vegas is reckoned to be five feet ten inches, to have a thirty-seven-inch chest and hips, and to be twenty-three years old. Lacquered, curled, mascara'd, dyed, powdered, painted, varnished, scented, shaved, costumed, jewelled, this size and shape of high-stepping strutter is known to be the perfect counterpoint to the non-stop gambling; to make card-tired eyes open. Las Vegas is in essence a man's town where the women are adjuncts to the masculine fun. Gambling is a kind of virility test, and American men gamble with gusto, in a way that few Europeans can or do. They have money to burn, and the girls are there to add to the fun, glittering fantasy girls.

But when, in even young women, a certain tautness goes, a maturity that would elsewhere be admired and loved sets in, Las Vegas is cold and its women have to be annealed. There is a steady stream of new, young and lovely starstruck girls offering themselves as recruits for the shows, so that slightly older women, even in their twenties, feel themselves prematurely aged, up against constant competition, insecure. Their worth is measured by their youthfulness, their vivacity, their callipygous quality, and the condition of their bosoms; so that, after a while, many join their predecessors in the search for cosmetic surgery of all kinds. And Las Vegas has its own clinic specializing in what is known as breast enhancement. Showgirls, cocktail waitresses and the sad shills all rely on their veneers and coachwork. There are few jobs in Las Vegas for women who no longer measure up, and this kind of insecurity contributes to one of the highest rates of suicide and alcoholism in the United States.

Prostitution is another important way in which women in Las Vegas earn a living. There are about four thousand in the city and the ready availability of them, as well as the great variety of pleasures they hint at in advertisements, no doubt contributes to Las Vegas' claim to be the entertainment capital of the world. The Las Vegas *Mirror* reminds its readers that prostitution is illegal in the city and in Clark County in which Las Vegas stands; but it carries a fat pull-out section with display advertisements for prostitutes. Direct to your room. We accept any credit card. All our escorts have health certificates. Bordellos are outside the city and county limits and offer to ferry clients to the ladies in their large display advertisements. For example: Sheri's Ranch, Nevada's most talked-about brothel, only sixty-three miles from Las Vegas, free limousine service leaves 10 a.m. 3 p.m. 8 p.m. 1 a.m. Judy's Coyote Spring Ranch Brothel: water beds, large selection of girls, Mastercharge. Grand opening: Desert Flower Ranch, Nevada's first-class brothel.

Important Notice! warns another paper, *This Week*. 'The unaware single gentleman can get himself into an area that can prove to be more than just a little embarrassing. There has been a recent influx of prostitutes, following a strong vice campaign in Southern California. This has put a lot of ladies on our streets. What the unwary man may think of as an easy pickup, can very often be a disaster in female form. More than one trusting soul has been tapped on the head only to find his bank roll missing. You also run a heavy risk of venereal disease. How do you explain that one to the wife or girlfriend? They'll never buy that old toilet seat story. The chance of your arrest is also a distinct possibility. In recent months, busts have been made where men have mistakenly propositioned a female vice officer. Try explaining that one to your company's board of directors. We have a number of licensed escort services advertising right here in *This Week*. If companionship is what you seek, why not go about it in a safe manner? Hell, you'll even find our escort services will be willing to take your credit cards.'

Tallest, biggest, fattest, strangest. It is said that gamblers still put plastic casino chips in the collection plates of the churches of Las Vegas. Dollars, of course, can be popped into the nearest slot machines on the way back to the hotel just in case a few minutes of pew-time should earn a jackpot.

Las Vegas is unique, thank heaven. It is a relief to take a shower and drive out across the baked desert and leave it and its surly people to their unremitting and unsmiling pursuit of money. As I set off I did not look back in case I was struck into salt.

8
THE SERGEANT

In the spongy, fat-haunched manner of large American cars, our white Chevrolet Impala oozed easily into the light traffic of a cold November evening and headed towards the shore of Lake Michigan. Sergeant Ronnie Watson pushed the wiper switch to flick rain-drops from the screen. This was the start of a routine supervisory patrol in the Chicago First Police District. It covers part of the Lake Michigan shore and the commerce and finance district within The Loop, which shares its nickname with the overhead railway system, the elevated metro on which the trains clank and rumble. The car we were in had the familiar police roof lights and a blue stripe along its flanks with the inscription *We Serve and Protect*.

'First thing,' the sergeant said, 'no auto chases in The Loop. None of that crazy stuff any more, like you see on TV. It's our commander's policy. We've lost good guys doing that. We had two good guys chasing a tearaway and they smashed into a truck. The End. You don't arrest nobody if you drive so fast that you don't ever get there. So we try to be more clever and block the roads. Sure, we have to hurry a little at times, but we don't go crazy.'

Sergeant Watson, slim and bespectacled, wore a badged cap and a dark blue zipped windcheater with his name tag on the chest. He was easy-mannered, laconic and relaxed. But he was also alert and ready: his eyes in a swift and practised manner

88

monitored the pavement, buildings and traffic. Occasionally he spoke into the radio clipped to his windcheater and listened to the background stream of messges and instructions flowing into and out of the control room. As a sector sergeant he was making a supervisory patrol of his beat and beside him on the seat was a clipboard log and worksheets. Beside him there was a torch and a long truncheon, his billy. He was also armed with a .38 Smith and Wesson revolver.

'When you join the Chicago police they swear you in and they loan you a star and a shield. You get a uniform allowance of three hundred dollars a year, half paid in January and the rest in August. We have to buy our own weapons and we do that through a regular dealer. The weapon has to be a .38 or .357 Colt or Smith and Wesson. That's standard. And we have to go through revolver training. In this district the commander doesn't like his policemen wearing too many guns. It isn't good for the image and these days we're trying to improve our image. You know all that stuff about cops in Chicago having a bad image a few years back, cops being on the take and all that. Anyway, there's no advantage in carrying a great armoury. When a police officer gets caught in a shoot-out it nearly always happens in a few seconds at a range of a few feet. Most gun battles are like that: short, nasty and close. There's no need to carry a lot of weapons. There wouldn't be time to use them. But you can carry an auxiliary if you want to; an automatic. And this can only be a Smith and Wesson or Browning 9 millimetre, or a Colt .45 or .38. But you have to qualify with automatics every year and carry a card saying that you are qualified.

'The automatic is not a good weapon. It's tricky to use effectively and it can be unsafe. As it happens, I own a .45 automatic, but I don't like it.'

Sergeant Watson joined the police force as a cadet when he was eighteen. 'When I left high school I was offered a book-keeping job. There were two different rates of pay. Blacks got ten dollars a week less than whites for doing the same job. That made me upset and disillusioned. I just drifted off to shoot pool for six months. Then my father saw this advertisement in the paper for police cadets and he said I should do something about it. He always said you can't sit on your ass thinking the world owes you a living. There are blacks who say: Hey, they owe us this, they owe us that, because we were enslaved, because we still get treated badly. Well, I know all about that feeling. I understand it. Blacks still get a bad deal and life is tougher for blacks. If you're black you've got to be that much better. I know what makes black people angry. I've been angry myself. But slavery has gone. I know that my people were slaves. I won't forget that, but I won't let it make me bitter either. My father said: God gave you the same as a white man, a brain. So use it. He said: The world owes you nothing. My father went to school and got to fifth grade and he told me to go further, and three of us kids finished high school.'

We drove out to Lake Shore Drive, past the Soldier Field football stadium where the Chicago Bears play, and across to Merrill Meigs airport, a finger of land in the lake. We parked, facing north. The rain had stopped. The city glowed and its lights shimmered in the waters of the yacht harbours and the Lake Michigan littoral. 'Ain't that something?' the sergeant said. It was magnificent. 'I don't ever tire of looking at it. It's a great city, Chicago, and not bad to live in either.'

Chicago's architecture is daring, stately and fine. The skyscraper was invented and perfected here, by the Welsh-American Frank Lloyd Wright, by Louis Sullivan and John Wellborn Root, and others. New York later became Skyscraper City in the world's imagination, but Chicago was the proving ground for building genius and still sets a certain style in clean and soaring buildings. The grandfather buildings, like the red-brick Monadnock of 1891, the Rookery of 1886, the Auditorium of 1889 are dwarfed, only in height, not in visual appeal, by the moderns, the First National Bank, Marina City, the IBM Building, the Hancock Centre, the Standard Oil Building, and the Sears Tower, the world's tallest building. Chicago's awesome new skyline has three of five tallest buildings in the world, all of them erected since 1970.

'Chicago,' the sergeant said, 'the trouble with Chicago is that it still has this bad name. You know, Al Capone, extortion, rackets, gangsters and all that. And the troubles of 1968, the Democratic convention, and the crowds on the streets, and the violence. But Chicago is really a great city. There are some nice areas where you can live and bring up your kids. Sure, there are bad areas too. The housing developments, the projects as they were called, just didn't work. They built apartment blocks, ten apartments on each floor, fifteen or sixteen floors, ten or twenty blocks on each site. A lot of poor people live in them and they aren't nice places. They're hard to police, too. Vertical policing, we call it: up and down in the elevators. It can get difficult.'

We moved back into the business district, Sergeant Watson watchful, speaking sometimes into his radio. The Loop area was much quieter now than it was during the day. 'A lot of the crime you get around here is window crashes, what you call smash and grabs. But there aren't many strong-arm robberies with weapons. Of course, Chicago is a big money place and there is still a lot of organized crime, and prostitution and gambling rackets, and a lot of the murders are the result of quarrels and trouble inside the crime organizations. Gang crimes are not often solved.'

The radio on his chest was squawking and he inclined his head to catch the message. Then he swung the wheel and accelerated. 'Let's go and see what's happening.' We drove to a car park close by the Michigan shore. A police car was there, and by it were two young patrolmen, one talking with a cigarette in his mouth and the other chewing furiously. In the back of their car, behind a wire grille, was a pale spotty young man looking sorry for himself.

The sergeant asked what had happened.

'Sarge, we were patrolling these parking lots and driving right by here real quiet when we heard this sort of low hissing noise. Sssssss. We stop by this car here and the air is coming out of the rear tyres. We get down and look under the axle and it's got bricks under it. As the air comes out the car settles right down on the bricks. We look around and see this dude in the next car. He's lying flat in the front seat, so we don't see him. But we see him. We go to the back of his car and inside it are more bricks and a wheel wrench with a stud [a nut] still in it and studs from the other car are all over the ground. We've been looking for this dude for a couple of weeks now. We've been getting complaints of wheels being stolen. Now we know how they do it. This dude has a shopping list. It gives the make and model of the cars from which the tyres and wheels are wanted.

He cruises round the parking lots, chooses his car, puts bricks under the axles and opens the tyre valves. Then he lights off with the wheels. He doesn't have to jack up the cars and there's no hard work. Here's the list we found in the dude's pocket.'

The sergeant said: 'A hundred dollars apiece for a wheel. Four hundred dollars a car. Several cars a night. It's big business.' He was pleased with the patrolmen's work and showed it. He agreed with them that the man in the police car cage could lead to the criminal behind the car spares racket.

'We'll bring in the dicks and a photographer. We want pictures of the bricks under the axle, of the bricks in the dude's trunk, of the wheel wrench with the stud in it. And we'll want one of the bricks, the wrench with the stud, and the shopping list retained for evidence.'

One of the patrolmen went off to radio for detectives and a photographer. I don't know quite what I had expected as an introduction to Chicago crime; probably something more violent and frightening, in keeping with television police melodrama, and Chicago's own reputation. It was interesting to note the policemen's enthusiasm for this relatively unexciting crime, the respect they had for the sergeant, and the sympathy they had for the driver of the car who arrived and asked what was going on.

'They're good policemen because they're interested in policing, which means getting to know about people and the area you work in, and developing an instinct for crime,' the sergeant said as we resumed our patrol. 'Those guys were observant. It seems a routine sort of crime, but their work can lead us on to busting something pretty big. This is a job unlike any other. No two nights are going to be the same. It's a job with risks, too. There's always a chance that one night you might not get home at all: you might run into some gunfire. Guns are always with us. I wear a gun every day of the year, and I have a gun around when I'm off duty, because even off duty I am still a police officer. The gun is there. I put it on just like putting my trousers on. But actually I don't hold with the right to bear arms. When the American constitution was written down there was a frontier and you might be attacked by a bear or something. Those days were different. And as long as we have guns in this country, easy to get in stores and in the mail, we will go on getting hurt. You get people shooting off those cheap imports, the Saturday night specials, little .22 guns that cause a lot of deaths. The .22 goes in and bounces around inside you, mashes you up, messes up your spleen and your liver and breaks your arteries.

'I would only use my gun to protect my life or yours. Our police department says you must use every available means of trying to capture before resorting to deadly fire. And deadly is what it is. A gun is not meant to wound. All that TV stuff about wounding. When you shoot at a person there's no one who's such an expert that he can shoot to wound. When a policeman fires he aims to kill.

'But I've never used my gun in anger. And I hope I never will.'

Chicago's police department, which has thirteen thousand officers aided by two thousand civilians, has, like the city's skyline, changed in the past few years. For decades, and especially during the long reign of the despotic mayor, Richard Daley, the police enjoyed little public respect: too many of them were cruel, careless, cynical bribe-takers and ruffians. They faked evidence and lied. Honest policemen tended to find it hard to get promotion. The bad ones were hard on Chicago's black people, abused them and beat them and neglected them. The police department's poor reputation was tarnished further by the bitter battles during the 1968 Democratic party convention. The balance of reports of those events is that the police went berserk. The police still say it's not true. (A Chicago police captain said to me, almost defiantly: 'I don't care what people say. We didn't riot. We're proud of what we did then. It was the end of the hippies. We did it for the whole country. We stood up to the rabble. And look at Chicago now. It's the safest large city in the United States and we have a good police department. Sure there are still corrupt cops. Every police force has them. I've been reading about your Scotland Yard. London police have a good reputation and everyone's heard of Scotland Yard, but you've still got your rotten apples.')

Sergeant Watson said: 'Discrimination has been fought in the Chicago police force and under new arrangements the promotion list has a proportion of sixty whites to forty minority people, and there's a new lieutenants' and captains' examination. It will take me another year to make lieutenant. I'm still going to school because education is the key to so much. I went to college when I joined the police. Then I had leave of absence for eighteen months because I was in the army in Vietnam. I worked seven years in the Third District until I was promoted sergeant. I went to school five nights a week, studying accounting and business administration. Now I've got my bachelor's degree and I'm studying for a master's degree in business administration. It helps a lot with the job. After all the police provide a service and it has to be run on efficient lines.

'I took a history course as well and learnt about the real history of America, about the blacks and the part they have played in American history.

'Now that blacks are being treated a little better, there is bound to be some resentment among some whites because they have to wait that little bit longer while blacks enjoy their fairer treatment. I've never let prejudice bother me. I've passed the examinations and earned my job. No one helps me. No nepotism, no favouritism, no old pals act. My qualifications are what count.

'But there, life is tougher for black people than white. Certainly tougher for black kids living in the tough neighbourhoods. It's hard for them to get into the unions, to get apprenticeships. Black kids still don't get a fair break. If only more employers and unions would give the black kids a break, they would make it. Whites still think they are better than blacks in the United States. It is bred into them. Many white people have never really met blacks, never shaken hands, never stepped into a black house.

'You know, we were the second black family to move into our street, and the whites next door decided to move out. The day they were moving the woman had to wait awhile, so my wife invited her in. She saw our place, with the nice furniture and the drapes. We'd got it looking really swell. And she was amazed. She thought black folks all lived in dirt. And she said: "Your home is beautiful. If I'd known that I wouldn't have wanted to move."

'As I say, we had the place looking nice, so I invited some of my colleagues round for a drink. No one came. So I said to them, look, I'm going to invite you just once more. So they made the step, they came to a black man's house. And you know what, they liked it. And their wives liked it, too. We all had a good time.

'So maybe things get better slowly. As for the police force, well the people we get in now are better educated. You have to have a high school education to get in now. And the money is fantastic, so that a man can feel well-treated and responsible. A patrolman gets fourteen thousand dollars a year to start with, twenty-two thousand after twenty-five years service. A sergeant gets twenty-four thousand, a lieutenant more than twenty-seven thousand and a superintendent forty-five thousand.'

We stopped at police headquarters and he offered to get a car to have me taken back to my hotel, but I said I would like to walk. 'One thing you can say,' he said, 'and maybe a few years back a lot of Chicago cops couldn't say it: there's a dignity in the job. I'm proud of being a policeman.'

9
BANG, YOU'RE DEAD

Buy a gun for your son right away sir!
Let his little mind expand,
Place a weapon in his hand.
                              Tom Paxton

On reflection, I suppose that the nearest I came to being shot in the United States was the evening in Texas, when I complained in a restaurant about the management watering the wine.

Normally I am uncomplaining in restaurants. But the watering of wine is to my mind an affront. On this occasion I was in a party of five or six people, one of whom had remembered that several years before he had had a fine meal in this particular restaurant. Unfortunately the restaurant was not the place it once had been. By the time we were ordering our dinner, the recommender realized that the management had changed and that the place was less savoury than in its former existence. A tired crooner stepped onto a small stage and began to sing in a strangled voice, as an accompaniment to the food which arrived in the kind of small portions that helpful restaurants serve for children. The arrival at the table of watered wine in bottles that had been opened elsewhere was a test of tolerance which I failed. I asked the waiter to bring unopened bottles and this he did with thunder in his face. At last the bill came and I noted that it included a full charge for the unconsumed watered wine and a gratuity of about forty per cent. One of our group threw down some dollars to meet the extortion, saying it was best to leave at once, and the waiter pocketed them. I, however, called for the manager.

The manager was broad-shouldered and hulking in an

96

ursine way. He had a large scowling face with a deep blue five o'clock shadow. He was wearing a short and curly blond wig, a delicate blue eye-shadow and a smart black cocktail frock. He had the sort of voice which would have suited a bear with a sore throat.

'Some problem with you guys?' he growled, glaring from beneath his blue lids.

'The wine was watered, the food terrible and expensive and the bill is robbery,' I offered.

His brow furrowed. His lips shrivelled like salted snails. A hush fell and the area around us darkened as three or four figures oozed forwards and blotted out the light. In this some-what sinister penumbra those of us who were left felt vulner-able. It was the moment in the western when the piano player stops playing and the bartender removes the bottle of Old Redeye whiskey and ducks down.

'Well,' the manager said evenly, fingering his twinkling brooch, 'there is no money back in this establishment. House rule.'

The look of menace on his face made it clear that it was time to retreat. Next morning I felt that that had been a sensible move. I read in one of the newspapers that in an argument over a bill in a Texas restaurant a man had been shot dead. House rule: difficult customers will be shot.

Better smarting than bleeding. I wondered if the grizzly in the restaurant had had a pistol alongside his corkscrew and swizzle stick; or down the front of his little black dress.

2

The privately owned handgun is perhaps America's saddest motif. It is the essential accoutrement of the tradition of violence and to many Americans it is one of life's necessities. To some men there is something mystical and almost holy about the gun and it has become an object of veneration. It seems a teddy for grown-ups, an object coddled and cradled and comforting. For some men it is part of manliness, apparently transmitting to its owner some of its potency. It is for them the adjunct of the firm jaw, the masculine hat and the manly swagger and manner. The acquisition of it is as much a part of growing up and of *machismo* as the descent of testicles.

Guns are what are in the minds of a fair number of American men when they think of strength. And to these men the exerting of strength is very important. A gunless moral courage is not in their concept of strength.

For people who come from a country whose citizens are unarmed and which has no tradition of firearms, the place of the gun in American life is inevitably a subject of morbid curiosity. In mainland Britain crimes in which guns are used, or the shooting of a criminal by police, are events which merit large headlines in newspapers because they are so rare. Americans still shake their heads in wonder when assured that British policemen do not carry firearms as a matter of routine. For our part, it takes a few days before we stop gaping at the sight of well-armed American cops, especially the big bulky ones with wet chewed cigars, sunglasses and aldermanic paunches held in place by a gunbelt. For many Americans the possession of a gun is unremarkable: they don't know what all the fuss is about. The guns on open sale, in shops and in advertisements, are as much a part of life as cars and hamburgers. This closeness to the machinery of violence is rather eerie to a stranger. The sheer scale of gun ownership is part of America's differential among the nations; to some Americans it is part of America's pride, but to others its shame; and the attitudes to firearms tells us something of the development and the values of American society.

A certain layer of reserve and restraint, and perhaps regard for human life, is in some respects thinner in the United States than it is, say, in Britain. For many Americans their country is a rough place and the frontier lives on, lawless and peopled by bandits and thugs. In their concept of strength, power lies in the trigger. At any sign of threat or pressure they reach for their guns. The gun is protection and assertion. If they want to show anger or determination or obstinacy they go to the rifle rack or the pistol drawer. If they want to ease their fear of being victims of burglary or assault they can send away for a gun for as little as thirty dollars or so. Their experience convinces them that they are right. The newpapers and television news bulletins are full of accounts of armed criminals and shot citizens. In an armed society, they reason, it is foolhardy not to be armed: the gun is the fast and sure way, better than policemen, better than argument, better than law, better than protracted persuasion.

In the mid-West farmers took out their guns to threaten their innocent fellow Americans who happened to be working on a government power-line crossing their land. Step on a farmer's land and you step on the corns of his soul. One Sunday morning, I asked a Sunday School teacher about the rights and wrongs of farmers threatening power-line workers. 'Sometimes,' she said, 'it seems the only thing that governments and bureaucrats understand is gunfire. It's wrong to go on people's land.'

But supposing, I said, a power-line worker were killed by a farmer. 'That would be the government's fault, not ours,' she said. 'We have to defend our rights.'

Rights. Americans talk a lot about rights, and to understand their feelings about rights helps in the understanding of America.

At the time the farmers were toting guns there was a coal miners' strike, and a number of miners damaged lorries and set up roadblocks. In response the mine owners turned their sites into armed camps. One boss spent six thousand dollars on guns for men who had not joined the strike and, who in defence of their right to go on working, were ready to use firearms. Another owner posted armed sentries at the mine entrance and worked with an automatic pistol on his desk and a grim expression on his face: the frontier lives.

One day in Alabama I got talking to the man who served me at a country store and petrol station. The conversation turned to crime and guns. 'No,' he said. 'Never had no stick-up here. It's a law-abiding little town. But you never can tell when some hoodlum might stop by and try to get a few bucks. So I got my Magnum for company, and that can make a big hole in someone's head.'

But when it came to the point, I said, would he actually level his revolver and pull the trigger. He thought it a strange question. 'Just try me,' he said. 'I'll do it all right.' He grinned. 'Any guy who gets one shot from my Magnum won't come back to have the job done over.'

There is in America a fascination with the tools of violence that, ingrained and powerful, is stronger than in almost any other country that regards itself as civilized. The roar of gunfire is tolerated as in no other society, and this is one of the disappointments of the American experience. In part, I suppose, the tradition of violence is rooted in the ruggedness of the nineteenth-century settlement of the west. It was America's adolescence and the romance of that epoch remains a strain in the American personality. The gun was firmly established: Colt and Winchester provided the technology, and with one at his hip and one in his hand a man could look westwards, protect his family, shoot his foes, hunt his game. The romance of man and gun became indelibly marked in the American progress. The gun was the friend of the Christian man, a weapon for God, America and freedom. And in times when the law straggled far behind the wagon trains, it helped to lay down the lines of a rough justice.

The violence of America was carefully chronicled; indeed no nation has so carefully recorded its own violence and obsession with it. Men would lynch a cowboy or a black man or Indian and then would pose for a team photograph around the gallows tree. They would prop shot men on boards to take their pictures: the dead were their trophies. Until I became an adult almost all my images of civilian violence were American ones. And after the photograph, the television picture: Jack Ruby shot Lee Harvey Oswald in the first live television murder. When the pathetic Gary Gilmore said he wanted to be shot by a firing squad in Utah the authorities would not make a stand for decency, but instead gave in to the public appetite for a ghoulish circus. Television companies wanted to film it, the modern equivalent of the gallows-side snap; and five thousand thrill-seekers volunteered to fire the bullets.

The frontier, though, can't be blamed for it all. Violence, as they say, is as American as apple pie and it grew from the clash of cultures, the freewheeling way of life with the old restraints chopped away, the growth and social heat of cities, migrations, despair, fear — and rights.

At the core of the question of violence in America is the matter of guns. That America has the most heavily-armed citizenry in the world, that many Americans are shot to death, is a source of concern and shame for a growing number of

Americans. But by no means for all. Discussions of guns, of licensing them or restricting them, strikes men where it is most sensitive: somewhere in their psyche it grates on their Americanness.

So you talk to people about violence and guns, and they nod and say sure, sure; and say how awful it all is. But then they will say: 'Aw, what the hell? if I want to have a gun why shouldn't I? It's my right to have it!'

It sounds, the first time you hear it, like the cry of a spoilt child; but it is deeper and more complex than that.

To broach the gun question is to touch a sensitive place. Unquestionably the gun is the prime tool of violence; but the argument today is to what extent the removal of the tool will reduce the violence. It is a labyrinthine argument and one littered with emotional quicksands. Crime statistics can be misleading and are fought over endlessly; but the firearm's place in crime and violence is beyond dispute. About every forty minutes someone in the United States is shot to death and about every two and a half minutes someone is the victim of an armed robbery. Seven-tenths of robberies are carried out by people armed with hand guns; and nearly half the murders in America are committed with hand guns. America is more murderous than any other modern industrialized society. Astonishingly so; among the two hundred and fifteen million people of the United States there are more than nine thousand murders a year committed with hand guns alone, fifty times more than are committed with guns among the more than two hundred million people in Britain, West Germany and Japan. In the ten years of America's war with Vietnam, more than twice as many Americans were shot at home, in the streets, in restaurants, in their places of work, than were killed in action.

There seems no limit to such stark illustrations. But so large is the growth in gun violence that figures quickly become outdated. The hammers fall on guns as fast as typewriter keys on paper.

Everybody knows this, and especially the manufacturers of firearms, to whom a rising crime rate is good news. Crime induces fear and a feeling that ownership of a gun is a sensible measure of self-defence. So people reach for a gun. And there, feeding the fear and feeding on it are the firearms manufacturers. There is a hand gun in half the homes in America, a rifle in seven-tenths. There is one hand gun for every four Americans and more than four new hand guns are sold every minute. But no-one really knows exactly how many guns are manufactured, imported and sold. The major gunmakers, Smith and Wesson, Colt, Ruger, Harrington and Richardson, High Standards, RG Industries, Charter Arms, Firearms Import and Export, and Sterling, operate as discreetly as undertakers and do not publish their sales figures. Most of them do not talk about their business, either; they will not discuss it with journalists and they do not give much help to the police and other authorities who would like to know more about the ways in which guns are marketed and how they are stolen and enter the criminal world. In a country where there is a pride in having everything open, where companies and government offices are willing to show you around, it is unusual to find such a large industry so secretive.

Guns are big business. In an analysis of money spent on recreational aids, guns are in third place, behind boats and photographic equipment. Today there are fifty million hand guns in civilian hands. In twenty years there will be twice that number.

The gun makers have much to gain by keeping the trade as unrestricted as possible, and something to lose if gun control laws are enacted and enforced. President Lyndon Johnson demanded an end to what he called 'the insane traffic in guns', and a police official who testified before a House of Representatives committee on crime, said that as far as firearms were concerned 'the issue at the national level is not one of crime...it is a question of commerce.'

The gun makers do not themselves join the battle directly. They keep, discreetly as ever, in the background. Their interests are represented by the National Rifle Association, the most important of the pro-gun organizations in America, which describes itself as the foremost guardian of the traditional American right to keep and bear arms. It is well-funded, its budget being about fifteen millon dollars a year, and it adopts an aggressive stance in the firearms debate. It is headquartered in a large and well-appointed eight-floor office block in Washington and has a staff of more than five hundred, many of whom are engaged in the countering of the gun-control arguments, in research and publicity. The asociation has a monthy publication, and also publishes pamphlets. It focuses on a single issue and knows the arguments inside out. It can mobilize spokesmen to appear on television and radio and can call on a large number of number of people to write to their senators and congressmen and to bring influence to bear in other ways. It has been most successful in blocking gun controls. It plays on fear, emotion and ignorance. And always, it talks of rights.

The National Rifle Association is *machismo* institutionalized. And a strong element in its activities and outlook is paranoia. It sees gun controllers as devils and well-poisoners, eroding the very tissue of their America. Its all-seeing eye watches the crannies of America for signs of gun controllers under the beds. Thus the association's magazine *American Rifleman* reported:

'Following Indiana's rejection of their English textbook series because of anti-gun, anti-hunting bias, publishers MacDougal Littel have sought National Rifle Association aid to bring balance into the texts. Indiana parents were excited to an inspired campaign against the textbooks which will be reissued with the biased material either deleted or balanced.'

In the same issue was a report about a government plan to destroy three hundred thousand rifles. To the gun lobby the idea of breaking up a gun is an outrage, so the NRA moved into action. This report shows how it can mobilize its members. 'A mailing to members in districts with Congressmen on the Armed Services Committees, and a radio alert to some seven hundred stations resulted in a public and Congressional outcry that forced the Defense Department to stop the destruction.'

Meanwhile the magazine runs a regular column called *The Armed Citizen*, which is a collection of news clippings illustrating the belief that guns are indispensable in the continuing fight against crime. A typical example: 'Phyllis Brown was behind the counter of the Stafford County, Va. store where she works when a man entered, pulled a gun, and demanded a hundred dollars. Instead, Mrs Brown pulled her own gun. The bandit quickly fled.'

In the letters column a Texas farmer writes: 'Owing to ease of access, durability, reliability and convenience, the farmers and ranchers of my aquaintance prefer a hand gun to any other type of firearm when they are working in the field or pasture. They consider the hand gun to be a very valuable tool in their business of providing food for a growing nation and a hungry world.'

And another correspondent wonders if God is doing enough for the gun: 'I think it is time for gun owners to try to get our churches to help us in our fight to keep and bear arms. If we lose our right to keep arms we will also lose our freedom of speech and our freedom of religion.'

Naturally enough, the magazine has hundreds of advertisements for guns and accessories; and also for bits and pieces of decoration like a belt buckle with a rifle motif and the slogan: 'I Will Give Up My Gun When They Pry My Cold Dead Fingers From It.'

You can also buy a belt buckle with the NRA's eagle holding a shield inscribed with the words the association never tires of citing: The Right To Bear Arms.

This is the second amendment to the constitution of the United States, and says in full: 'A well-regulated Militia, being necessary to the security of a free state, the right of the people to keep and bear Arms shall not be infringed.' In the interpretation of the National Rifle Association the amendment has the quality of holy writ. The amendment, though, is an anachronism and, as the Supreme Court has ruled, does not confer a constitutional right of arms-bearing on every American citizen. But sophistry is part of the NRA's stock-in-trade and the second amendment is constantly paraded.

Certainly Harlon Carter, vice-president of the association did so when I met him in the NRA offices in Washington. Mr Carter, a barrel-chested Texan, quoted not only the amendment, but also the Bible to make the case for unlimited guns. 'Any proposal to have guns registered is an invasion of privacy, a sinister and dangerous thing,' he snorted. 'The argument about hand guns is not about the length of a gun barrel, but about the whole panorama of liberty. What sort of society will we have if we throw it away and allow gun controllers to restrain and restrict? Every home owner has the right to be armed against the invader. Every law-abiding American has the right to own his gun. Why should that right be jeopardized just because one hundredth of one per cent offend the law. Everyone agrees that the press should be free, but millions of people die every decade because of what the press says. We all think it's worth it, don't we, for the freedom. Gun control adds up to one thing: the private citizen will be at the mercy of government agencies. Our freedom and our rights will vanish.'

He began to rant and hit the table. 'We will not give up our rights. The gun controllers want to eliminate guns and drive people out of business and out of jobs. The ordinary citizens will be at the mercy of the criminals. And why blame the gun? Guns don't cause crime. People do.'

This is a theme of the National Rifle Association. It is briefly stated, facile and effective. The innocence of the tool is a well-polished argument, and the NRA urges attention to the roots of crime, steering attention away from guns and towards the evidence that, as the jargon has it, socio-economic factors are to blame — and that, more particularly, black people are involved in crime to a much greater extent than whites. The association says that blacks are more often the killers and robbers, and blacks are more often the victims of gun violence. The implicit question in the association's argument is: why should the right of decent law-abiding white citizens to have guns for their recreation and self-protection be imperilled by a small criminal minority, mostly black? And it comes back to the original point: a gun no more kills than a reporter's type-writer commits a libel.

The analogy and argument are dubious. The use of a revolver requires no intellectual input, the trigger can be pulled in an instant of greed, madness, fear, jealousy or callousness, and there is no scrutiny or check on a bullet leaving a muzzle at three thousand feet a second. Leaving that aside, I doubt that a gun is an entirely innocent contraption. It inspires an extra-ordinary worship, as evidenced by the gun publications, and to many people there is something potent, almost magical, in its ability to deal death anonymously from a distance. A gun demands use and proof of its power. Its existence raises the base-line of violence. When I was a small boy I once spent half a spring morning with an older boy who had an air rifle. He would creep up on foraging blackbirds and thrushes and shoot them. Their eyes would close and they would fall over gently. 'I love to see them falling over,' he breathed. His eyes were bright. One reason why the gun control lobby is active is because there are some people who like to see other people, even innocent strangers, fall dead at their hands.

There is an argument that gun control, the enforced registration of hand guns and a stricter licensing and gun dealing system, is merely dealing with the symptoms of violence and not its causes. Of course, there is something in this; but I would guess that the fact that guns are as common as doughnuts is an important ingredient in American violence. Even if this were demonstrably not true, the small but persistent lobby for the control of hand guns is important because it offers a society perplexed by, ashamed of, and frightened by, its violence an opportunity to *do* something, to do *something*. Opinion surveys have shown that nearly three-quarters of the American people favour some kind of gun registration law, a law requiring people to obtain police permits before being allowed to buy weapons. The reaction from the NRA to such ideas is shrill and vehement. In 1979 President Carter was forced by the outcry manipulated by the NRA to back down from his promise of action on gun control; and the gun manufacturers breathed again. A former Attorney-General of the United States once remarked: 'Show me a man who doesn't want his gun registered, and I will show you a man who shouldn't have a gun.' The NRA's retort to that, in the modern bumper stickers, is When Guns Are Outlawed Only Outlaws Will Have Guns. And so the argument goes on. Harlon Carter, the NRA chief, says: 'For those of us who own and use guns, gun control is a gut-wrenching matter ... ' And so it is for those who want to make a start on eroding America's tradition of violence. They say gun control would be such a start: imperfect, difficult, but at least action rather than hand-wringing. Laws cannot easily get to the roots of violence, any more than laws on racial discrimination can make black people love white people and vice versa. But laws can provide a framework in which minimum levels of decency and behaviour can be observed; they can help to create a climate and reinforce a more civilized standard of relationship. Years before he became president,

Abraham Lincoln described internal violence as the greatest threat to American political institutions. One hundred and forty years later there is still truth in that statement.

'I will Give Up My Gun When They Pry My Cold Dead Fingers From It.' There was a sense of relief when I had finished my interview at the National Rifle Association. The rhetoric stopped and Harlon Carter and his colleagues said they had enjoyed the meeting and hoped I would have a nice day. They gave me a NRA lapel badge with the slogan: Freedom.

About two months later, in San Francisco, I was invited to dinner, with other journalists, to talk about the problems associated with governing that marvellous city. Our host was Harvey Milk, a camera shop owner, who was on the city's board of supervisors, or governing body. He was a homosexual who made no secret of his homosexuality when he campaigned for office. San Francisco has a considerable proportion of homosexuals in its population and Mr Milk achieved office by promising to represent their interests, as well as the interests of others. He said that he had been the first person to speak frankly of his homosexuality and get elected. He had made the homosexual community think of politics and issues and he thought his honesty had helped to make homosexuality respectable in that city. 'I get on well with a lot of people. I try to do my job. I think that bringing homosexuals into politics in this honest way has been healthy for the community. It is ceasing to be remarkable. But some people don't like it. They are afraid and they can't cope with it. Sure there are people who don't like me, don't like what I've done. And being in public life has its dangers. I know that. Everybody knows that. This is a violent country and guns are plentiful and easy to get. Lots of people get shot, people in public life. If you are in the public eye and people don't like you they can take a shot at you. It's the sort of thing we do in America. Kennedy. King. Kennedy. Wallace. Lots of people. I've no doubt that some day some guy will get me.'

He smiled a lazy smile. 'I guess it's on the cards.'

Some time later, when I was back in Britain, I heard that a man had gone into the San Francisco city hall and had killed the mayor and Harvey Milk with a hand gun.

10
PRESS HERE FOR ARMAGEDDON

On February 20, 1971, the National Emergency Warning Center issued a teletyped warning to all radio and television stations ordering them off the air and to operate under the elaborately preplanned conditions for communicating to a population in the event of nuclear war. Investigation disclosed that the wrong tape had been fed into the transmitting machine. Said the operator, who had worked at the center 15 years, 'I can't imagine how the hell I did it.'
Seymour Melman, *The Permanent War Economy*

I did not much like the look of the military policeman, and I supposed he did not much like the look of me. He was stocky and bulky, but the bulk was plainly hard muscle and I doubted there was a half-ounce of cellulite on him. He was a human projectile; his father had been concrete and his mother iron. His eyes were flint and his jaw granite and I knew that under his helmet his hair would have been steel wool one quarter of an inch long. He had the aggressive mien of a bull and I imagined he never smiled in duty hours and perhaps never at all, regarding it as a sign of weakness. He looked supremely fit and intimidatingly tough. He carried a gun, of course, but on his deadly-looking frame it seemed a superfluous decoration; no doubt he knew how to deliver a dozen fatal blows with his hands.

He looked at me hard and said: 'Just a warning. If there is an alarm get your back against the wall and freeze. I have a job to do and if that alarm goes I will have to get to the end of this corridor as fast as I can. So do not stand in my way. If you are in my way I will not stop. I will run right through you.'

I believed him. He was like everyone at the Strategic Air Command headquarters near Omaha, Nebraska: serious, purposeful and clearly dedicated. The people who work here have their hands on the firing mechanism of the United States' nuclear weapons. Some have their hands on the safety catch and some have their hands on the trigger.

Strategic Air Command, founded 1946, motto: Peace is Our Profession, defines itself in these words: 'SAC contributes to the deterrence of war, particularly nuclear war, by providing ready, flexible and credible strategic offensive forces capable of responding decisively across a spectrum of threats to the vital security interests of the United States.' It means that every day the people who work under SAC's control take every carefully controlled step on the road to war, except the last one or two. Given a certain set of numbers and letters, certain orders in a pre-ordained, well-rehearsed macabre ritual, these people, as surely as robots, would pull the toggles, turn the keys and press the buttons that would send the missiles and the bombs to incinerate our planet. Strategic Air Command headquarters is not a secret place. The rooms where its people would swiftly act out the parts for which they are trained, and 'become Death, the destroyer of worlds', can be visited by groups of interested citizens. It is part of American openness: it belongs to the people, so the people should be able to see it. Probably the citizens are impressed, satisfied that the dollars they pay for defence spending are well spent, that they are, as the slang has it, getting a bang out of a buck.

The headquarters building sits beside a well-kept sweep of grass, and by its front door are trees, flag masts and a tall white intercontinental ballistic missile, not in working order, and, by ICBM standards, an antique. There are three floors above the ground, a basement, and three floors deep below ground which are contained in a concrete box with walls two feet thick. In emergency the underground section can be sealed off and a community of eight hundred souls could exist for weeks, presumably emerging when the ultimate war is won and lost, to pick their way through the cinders. Forty-six feet below the ground is the command post, one hundred and forty-nine feet long and thirty-nine feet wide. It is filled with consoles and telephones and buttons; and on one wall are six display screens, each sixteen feet by sixteen feet on which is displayed, in seven colours, a mass of information about aircraft targets, movements, weapons and weather. It is from this continuously manned room that, on receipt of a coded message from the President, the missiles and bombs would be launched.

The bombs are in the B52 bombers, stationed throughout the country, always loaded, always ready. Their crews live close beside their aircraft and they can have the engines started within ninety seconds of an alert and be ready for take-off within five minutes. They fly to orbiting points well outside enemy territory and eventually return to base. They would only continue to their targets if they received what is called the Go Code. Meanwhile, always in the air, is a Strategic Air Command Boeing 707, a flying command post which duplicates the underground war room in Nebraska. These planes fly in eight-hour shifts and they have been airborne continuously since February of 1961.

On the ground, always ready too, are the teams responsible for the maintenance and launching of more than a thousand Minuteman and Titan missiles which lie polished and poised in silos scattered throughout the United States. A Titan crew consists of two officers and two airmen, a Minuteman crew of two officers, and they serve four years as missile crews working in twelve-hour shifts. They are extraordinarily dedicated men and women, and even Strategic Air Command refers to them as 'aggressive individuals.' It is not possible for one member of the crew to fire a missile, for, among other checks and counter-checks, there are separate keys which have to be turned simul-taneously. The crews are screened frequently to see that their minds remain balanced, and they carry guns. If one of the crew has a breakdown and seems to be going off his head, his buddy is under orders to kill him.

I wondered, if it came to the point, how many would tremble, or draw back, from the bombtits and doom toggles, or run white-faced from the room. People I met at Strategic Air Command thought that training and selection took care of that kind of worry; and as for themselves they said they had no doubt that what they were doing was right. They were doing it, they said, for their families and America and, dammit, for a lot of people.

110

I understood their point of view.

But even when I saw that eerie execution chamber of a war room, deep underground, with its soft lights and paraphernalia and its staff of frowning, committed men and women, vetted for stable minds and patriotism, I found it difficult to believe that it was the real thing. It seemed too alien. I knew, as they told me, that what they did was necessary; and I supposed that, as a west European, I should have felt gratitude. But when I looked at this place I experienced a sense of futility; for these obedient people are schooled to perform the unspeakable and unimaginable, to destroy utterly when hope has vanished.

11
SIPPIN' WHISKEY

Freedom and Whisky gang thegither!
Robert Burns

There is not one America, of course, but many. To foreigners the best-known facets are the wild open butte-knobbed landscapes of the west and the constantly limelit cities like New York, Washington and San Francisco. But there is another, more private and gentler America, the countryside of wooded valleys and small towns and villages. Life here is not paced by digital quartz watches, but by clocks of stately dowager tick. Life is busy enough, and fulfilling enough, but it is also paced properly so that there are enough spaces in the day for the pleasures of conversation, reflection, idle staring, the careful lighting of pipes, whittling of sticks and decent eating.

City dwellers and people in transit feed as they go, like aircraft refuelling in mid-air. They grab a hamburger and masticate it quickly and nervously, as if they had stolen it: they wolf like thieving foxes. In the country the people like a plate in front of them and something properly cooked upon it, and a chair under them long enough for it to get warm: city folk never seem to sit long enough to get a good shine on their trousers.

The humour is different, too, in spite of coast-to-coast television and its imposition of uniformity. The cities are still the places for quick gags and forgettable one-liners and the pithy jokey insults of taxi-drivers. In the country there is a humour redolent of the gentle leg-pulling and deadpan shaggy-dog stories of Wales and parts of rural England and Scotland.

112

It is a humour that tickles shyly and many of the tales have a matured flavour of chestnut, to which I am partial. It is a home-cured mirth that satisfies.

In the foothills of the Cumberland Mountains, in middle Tennessee, there is a small town where they have this unfrenetic outlook and warm dry humour. I found it beside Mulberry Creek as I drove along Davy Crockett Highway, about seventy miles south-east of Nashville. Crockett homesteaded hereabouts between 1811-13 before going into politics as a congressman; and at about that time groups of settlers began to put down their roots by Mulberry Creek. They found, however, that their peace and their labours were disturbed by local bandits who had different ideas of free enterprise, and this irritated them. As was the fashion of those days the settlers took matters into their own hands and, after the manner of Charles Lynch, the Virginian planter who gave his name to the practice, lynched the neighbourhood malefactors on a fine large beech tree. Thus the town came to be known as Lynchburg and so it is called to this day, a handsome little place of smart white clapboard houses, with a store, petrol station, boarding-house, an old jailhouse, covered sidewalks, restaurant, a courthouse and a Confederate war memorial, all nestling among thick copses and grassy patches. The sign at the side of the road informs that its population is three hundred and sixty-one.

Lynchburg has a certain fame and owes it to a little fellow of five foot two, and a choleric glare, called Jack Daniel, who, unfortunately, kicked himself to death.

It was an unusual thing to do, even in Tennessee; but before he aimed the kick Mr Jack, as he was known, had placed Lynchburg firmly in the affections of many Americans, where he still is. For he spent his lifetime manufacturing and perfecting Jack Daniel's Old Time Tennessee Sour Mash Whiskey, distinguished by its square bottle, its black and white label, and, of course, its flavour and its way of inducing gentle embers in the brain and making the ears roseate. The Jack Daniel distillery is the oldest legal one in the United States and has a plaque on the clapboard wall of Mr Jack's old office, where he actually kicked himself to death, certifying that the manufactory is on the government's register of historic places and therefore deserves preservation as part of the cultural heritage of the United States. And so it does. Quite properly, too, there is a note in the Congressional Record, repository of many famous utterances, recording a tribute paid to the whiskey by a Tennessee senator. It strikes just the right note: 'One of the most celebrated liquors in our state, and indeed one of the most celebrated liquors in the country is manufactured at Lynchburg. It is called Jack Daniel. Mr Daniel was a splendid man, and he began the manufacture of a liquor which I am told is peculiarly enticing and attractive to anyone who tastes it.'

The senator, mindful of the teetotal vote in the state, did not actually say, you note, that he himself was a taster of the beautiful brown sour mash. But even the sternest of Tenesseean teetotallers looks at the distillery in perspective: everybody knows that it is the second largest federal taxpayer in the whole state. And that is why the government keeps a record of every drop distilled and a government man has a key to all the vital stores in the distillery.

Jack Daniel's Old Time Tennessee Sour Mash is not at all the Old Tennis Shoes that John Steinbeck wrote of. It is considerably more aristocratic than that. It is not a bourbon; it is a true Tennessee whiskey from a mash of cooked cornmeal to which is added rye and barley malt, and then some yeast, and then some mash from the previous brew. It is the adding of this last ingredient which makes the whole mash a sour mash. And then, to render it smooth, the distilled liquid drips through vats of sugar-maple charcoal twelve feet high. This is the mellowing process — and after it has gone through that the 'enticing' liquid is aged in oak casks for at least four years.

It is known as sippin' whiskey, an appellation which evokes a picture of companionship, rocking-chair conversation and contemplation. Though what else you could call a good whiskey but sippin' whiskey, I don't know: unless there is a gulpin' whiskey. Anyway, having sipped a glass or two of it elsewhere in America, I felt it right to pay a visit, and I went, as pilgrim to a shrine, to the Jack Daniel Distillery Number One. As it happens, there isn't a Number Two.

After I had signed the visitors' book the receptionist looked at the address and said kindly that if I had come all the way from England I could not possibly go round the distillery without having lunch first. So I was to go down the street until I came to a big old white house on the left, and to go right in and have some lunch, and while I was on my way the big old white house would be telephoned and I would be expected.

Lunch was at Mrs Bobo's boarding-house, known locally as the Bobo Hilton, a handsome tree-shaded house with a pillared front porch and a balcony. Mrs Bobo was tiny and bright and told me she was ninety-seven, so she was a little younger than the boarding-house. The house dates from the Civil War, or what many people in the former Confederate states still refer to as 'the war between the states.' Mrs Bobo directed me to a long table where there were some other guests, and we all had a lunch of baked macaroni, broccoli and cheese sauce, green beans, white beans, cornmeal mush with cheese, fried chicken, casserole beef, coleslaw, chicken with apple and cinnamon, cornbread biscuits and, to finish, apricot roll and ice cream with iced tea. Mrs Bobo asked how I had enjoyed southern cooking and she beamed when I said: 'Hugely.'

At the door she waved goodbye. 'You all come back now,' she said.

Back at the distillery there was a guide waiting to take a small group of us around. His face was deadpan but its creases were made by laughter. How, I asked, did Lynchburg's population of three hundred and sixty-one, as displayed on the road sign, remain constant.

'Now that's real observant, and it's a funny thang. Ever' time a gal hereabouts has a baby, some man gits up and leaves town.' He made everyone feel like the feed to his stand-up comic.

He took us round Jack Daniel Hollow — Old Holler — where the distillery sits and drips the dark golden stuff. Sugar maple logs are split and burned in the rickyard to make the charcoal for filtering. This lasts for five or six months in the filtering vats. 'It's up to the whiskey taster. When he says the charcoal has to be changed, then it is changed. And the old charcoal is made into briquettes and used as fuel. You can do hamburgers over it in a barbecue, and you wake up next morning with a hangover.'

The water used in the distillery is taken from a limestone

spring in the hollow. Its purity and constant temperature is the reason why Jack Daniel set up in business in Lynchburg in the 1860s. Close to the spring is a statue of Mr Jack, erected soon after his mortal kick in 1911. It shows him in his habitual hat and looking rather bad-tempered. 'Jack Daniel has been stoned since 1911,' the guide said, gathering us round the life-size statue for a group photograph. 'Now if this picture comes out we'll send you a copy, and if it doesn't we'll send you a copy anyways. All you have to do is make sure you're standing next to who you should be standing next to; or you'll be meeting the mailman for the next three weeks.'

In the distillery, with its lovely heavy aroma, we stood around a fermenting vat and the guide invited us to dip our noses over the rim and take a deep sniff. The effect was stunning. The fumes seemed to scour the skull clean of brain and the eyes popped and watered. The guide gave a slow smile as he watched our suddenly jerking heads and heard the gasps. 'If anyone had sinus trouble, he ain't got it now!' After inspecting the mellerin' process, in the mellerin' vats, we went to see Mr Jack's old office, now abandoned, but left exactly as it was years ago, with old ledgers and receipts and calendars. And there it was, with an old besom leaning against it, Mr Jack's iron safe. And this is how it happened: one day he found he couldn't get the safe open and, being short-tempered, flew into a rage and gave it a hefty full-back's kick. But he damaged his foot so badly that an infection set in and he died of his injury.

As they say in the distillery: 'If only he would have kicked somebody in the britches instead, he'd probably still be alive today.' But never mind, his legacy lingers on in countless palates.

And here's the rub. When you leave the distillery you get not so much as a thimbleful of a free sample. They give you all the lemonade you care to drink. But they cannot give you any of the 'peculiarly enticing' charcoal-mellered nectar. It's illegal. The county where the distillery stands, where once you could get a free ham lunch in a bar if you bought a glass of Jack Daniel, forbids the selling of spirituous beverages. You can't get a drop of it in the whole damned county! Your rueful laughter lasts you all the way along the Davy Crockett Highway and out of Tennessee.

116

12
CAN'T R.I.P.

It so happened that I crossed the broad Mississippi and entered Memphis on the occasion of Elvis Presley's first post-death birthday.

In death, as he was in his unquiet life, Mr Presley is the subject of immense morbid curiosity and the generator of a lot of dollars. Girls still stand, wet-eyed and twisting their handkerchiefs, outside the metal gates of his mansion on Elvis Presley Boulevard; and entrepreneurs and investors still bless his memory as they enter the bank. For them the fruit machine is jammed on jackpot as the Presley industry runs inexorably on, under the momentum of the five hundred million records that the singer sold in his lifetime. Elvis Presley has joined the small corps of the show business undead. Electronics and exploitation have made his death seem only a brief hiatus, a small twist in the stream of adoration and profit. But Mr Presley was in any case essentially superfluous to the Presley industry for some years before his death; his youthful best work was done long before, and he seems now, as he was in the unhappy years preceding his demise, neither dead nor alive, but somehow an oddity preserved; in abeyance, a fly in amber.

Given that, it is surprising that Mr Presley lies decently buried in the garden of his home in Memphis, beside the mother he adored: one almost expects to find him preserved under glass, like Lenin. And it is a relief to find that — bearing in mind that Albert Einstein's brain was preserved in a bottle after death — no mortal part of Mr Presley is on view; which says something about the simple good taste of his managers and exploiters. I confess I had half expected to find in Memphis a glass case displaying, perhaps, a plastic model of the famous pelvis. The swinging of this upset middle-aged and puritan America in the 1950s and led to a piquant Grundyish compromise when Mr Presley first appeared on nationwide television: he was said by Ed Sullivan to be unfit for family viewing, so when he performed on the Ed Sullivan Show the camera showed nothing below the waist. How quickly the older generation had forgotten its own antics over Rudolph Valentino and its disgraceful mob behaviour at political congresses.

Now, twenty-two years and a revolution later, there was a marking in Memphis of the late and virtually canonized singer's forty-third birthday. A bazaar was staged at the Everett R. Cook convention centre where, after paying two dollars and fifty cents to get in, solemn pilgrims snailed mournfully around stalls laden with Presleyana, while the songs of the late king were played continuously.

It takes a certain cool cheek to charge people to get into a costermongers' benefit and these mongers had it. A discerning curate might have disqualified some of the merchandise from the average church jumble sale on the grounds of junkiness. There were all manner of gewgaws, doodads and icons. There were pendants, watches and clocks with Mr Presley's darkly sulky features upon them, and his portrait was on teeshirts, scarves and pieces of black velvet. There were thousands of postcards, photographs and posters, and pictures that glow in the dark, mostly dating from the years when he bestrode the world of rock and roll and represented, with glowering sexuality and powerful stage energy, the restlessness and rebellion of the new generation. There were few pictures from the years of decline in Memphis when, fat, puffy and paranoid, strapping on a bullet-proof vest for his rare public appearances, he lived out what remained of his aimless and lonely life.

As well as souvenirs there were relics for sale. There was a pair of Mr Presley's shoes, dated with the year of wearing, though they were not blue suede ones. There were some gloves and motor-cycle gauntlets. A man sat beside a small table on which he had displayed a scarf labelled: 'Elvis gave me this, 1976. Best offer?'

On a stall there were brochures advertising an auction of some of the singer's possessions, including a Bible inscribed Elvis Aaron Presley. 'This keepsake,' the aution catalogue noted, 'confirms his deep religious reverence.'

Recalling the curls of Lord Nelson's hair I had seen in England, tastefully preserved in lockets, I wondered if any of Mr Presley's lacquered and dyed black curls had been snipped and kept for profit and for girls to moon over down the years. But I saw none. Once, a disc jockey offered as a prize seven of Mr Presley's hairs and within a few days received more than eighteen thousand applications. I noted in a survey of Mr Presley's life that his hair was lacquered so stiff that stones would bounce off it.

At one of the stalls a man handed me a copy of Mr Presley's last will and testament, its seven pages held in a neat blue folder. I was surprised when I was told there was no charge. I picked up a leaflet offering ' a part of Elvis's dream'. This was a deed of ownership of one square inch of the Presley ranch, the Circle G, for the equivalent of five pounds. Instead of buying I went across to a makeshift cinema where many of Mr Presley's thirty-three films were being shown without inter-ruption to audiences of women who sat sniffling into hand-kerchiefs or bolt upright with tears dribbling down their cheeks and splashing into their laps. Their sense of loss was evidently strong, and friends and neighbours in the cinema patted each other's arms and squeezed shoulders while, up on the screen, the immortal hips rotated.

As I left a man gave me ('No charge for a fan from old England, no sir') a reprint of the Memphis *Press-Scimitar* and the Memphis *Commercial Appeal* of Wednesday, August 17, 1977, reporting the death of their 'illustrious citizen' the day before. *'Death captures crown of rock and roll'* and *'A lonely life ends on Elvis Presley Boulevard'*, they said in their head-lines.

I went over to the boulevard, to see Gracelands mansion, Mr Presley's deathplace and gravesite. People were making their way up the curving drive in a steady stream, walking at measured mourners' pace on this, the great man's birthday. I heard that English admirers have paid five dollars apiece for pebbles from the drive. The pilgrims paused in front of the entrance porch. A large unshaven man was on patrol there, with a walkie-talkie radio. He had been one of Mr Presley's bodyguards, and he was retaining the job, post-mortem.

'So this,' one of the visitors said, rather unnecessarily, but unable to bear a hole in the conversation without trying to fill it, 'so this is Mr Presley's house.'

'Not quite sir,' the bodyguard said gently, with a note of deep reverence in his voice, 'this, sir, is Elvis's home.'

He holstered his radio and led the way to the grave, confiding that the recently discovered plot by criminals to steal the body and ransom it would never have succeeded because the copper coffin was fitted out with secret security devices. Mr Presley once had a Cadillac sprayed with a paint made of fish scales and diamonds and its metal trim parts plated with gold, and it was equipped with gold-plated telephones and a gold electric razor: what you give to the man who has everything is a tomb with a burglar alarm.

The grave was set in a circular walled and Doric-pillared plaza with a fountain playing in the centre. Standing sentinel was a large white statue which I took to be of Christ, though it had the word Presley inscribed on its plinth. All around the mausoleum and the adjoining swimming pool were wreaths and displays of flowers, many arranged on easel stands and made up in the shape of hearts or guitars, or the figure 43, the age Mr Presley would have been on this birthday. One flowery tribute was marked TCE: Taking Care of Elvis. The shrine was lush with flowers and damped with tears. The pilgrims paused in front of the grave and its bronze tablet, marked Elvis Aaron Presley. Women wept, perhaps mourning lost adolescence. A Chinese gentleman asked the Presley bodyguard if he might use a restroom and was given special permission to use the singer's poolside lavatory; a moving experience for any fan.

I called in at a theatre in Memphis to see part of a show called 'Elvis — the Legend Lives', the centrepiece of which was a performance by an unknown singer dressed up like Elvis Presley, complete with slicked black hair and crankshaft pelvis. He was one of the dozens of grisly show business clones,

120

some of whom are having plastic surgery the better to look like Mr Presley and to make money from the still grieving and gullible fans. On this occasion the impersonation was quite bloodless and attracted fewer than a hundred people.

'I'm really sorry you happened along here in Memphis on the day of that guy's birthday,' a businessman with whom I dined said. 'Sure there's a hell of a lot of people who are proud of Presley for the attention he brought to our city, and there's talk of building statues to him and big memorials and all that stuff. But there are a lot of decent citizens who think this sort of carnival is sick. Almost as sick as Presley was.'

He jerked his thumb towards Gracelands. 'Drugs, girls, booze — that's what went on over there. Behind the image Presley was a bad boy and I for one ain't proud of him. And there's something wrong somewhere when a few people are making a whole lot of money out of those sick souvenirs. Hell, he's bigger business now he's dead than when he was alive.'

Mr Presley, though, is secure. The young women at the gates of Gracelands who scrawl their messages of love on the wall, simply will not believe anything that shows their saint to be less than alabaster white. He was, and even in death still is, the founder-leader of a tribe, a phenomenon expressed simply in a TCE fan magazine editorial in this manner: 'By being together I feel we have all helped each other survive heartache which only a fellow Elvis Presley fan could understand. But we've made it, and it's my guess that we will continue to make it together just as long as we keep together. It's your duty as an Elvis fan to show everyone else that you still care…we know in our hearts that there will never be another Elvis.'

Just off Elvis Presley Boulevard there is a little restaurant where you can get ham and eggs and hush puppies quite cheaply and there is an individual jukebox on each table. Some of the tunes available are the usual third-rate country music and drab pieces like 'Who Wants A Slightly-Used Woman' and 'Slide Off Your Satin Sheets.' But mostly the records are Elvis Presley's. As the emblazoned teeshirts of the lachrymose fans say: 'The King Lives.'

13
NEW DIXIE

America is a tune. It must be sung together.
Gerald Stanley Lee

Almost imperceptibly, between one petrol fill-up and the next it seemed to me, the South began to seep into my consciousness like a slowly rising tide wetting a beach. The air grew warmer and the texture of the land and vegetation grew softer and lusher. Tobacco leaves hung like great kippers to dry in the sun, and wisps of cotton blew gently across the road from the plantations, to lie like soft snow along the verges. It was late October and the cotton, planted in April and May, was being harvested. In the shimmering fields the tall, red picking machines which, since the 1950s, have freed black people from their long drudgery, were steadily plucking the snowdrop blobs of cotton, and large mesh-sided trucks and trailers stuffed with cotton, like bursting cushions, were unloading at depots. There were cotton stacks with tarpaulin hats. Beside the road were occasional straggles and knots of humble clap-board homes, their mailboxes on tipsy posts; and on the porches old black men with greying hair sat and talked and took their midday ease, while nondescript dogs snoozed and scratched, and kids idled and scuffed in the dust and chickens pecked. Rows of faded blue jeans hung out to dry. At intervals there was an airstrip alongside the road, with little fat crop-spraying planes, and lazy windsocks; and the railway line seemed to run as straight as a lance to the horizon. There were wooden churches with smart white paint and wooden stores with peeled paint and faded Coke signs and old oil drums, with women and children and old men in bib overalls sitting and leaning in attitudes of languor. The warm air seemed to have a weight to it. The villages of white frame houses and small stores had a friendly and unhurried air; and I found that these were places of politeness. The voices were softer and the people broke even small words into drawled syllables, rolling each one around the mouth as if tasting claret. They savoured the language and said, not five, but faahv; not seven but say-uh-ven; not bread but bray-uhd; and I found the sounds tantalizing, believing I could detect a twang of Devon here and there, or little hints of Gloucestershire.

One sunny morning in Alabama I turned down a leafy minor road, found a small town and parked at a meter. It cost one cent for twenty-four minutes. Many small towns in America have parking meters: they don't really need them, but it is a kind of harmless municipal boast, a little status symbol. I went into a restaurant and store for breakfast. Breakfast is a cheap meal in America, except when taken in posh hotels in large cities, and you can get enough to eat and drink for ninety-nine cents in many places.

'How yuh doin'?' the waitress said brightly, coming to take my order. I said I was fine and that I would have black coffee, eggs over easy, grits and corn bread.

'Carf no cray-um, ay-igs over easy, gree-uts, corn bray-uhd,' she translated into southern. It is, as I say, a musical and relaxed language in which words are wrought into fascinating shapes. Southerners say that their speech is so measured that before a southern girl can explain that she won't, she already has. I wondered if news bulletins took twice as long to read in the South as in the North. And I found that one of the pleasures of the South is to listen to its people talking.

The speech of the South is only one of the many qualities that give the region its special flavour. Manners, outlook, the racial component, history, geography, architecture, agriculture and diet play their parts, too, in varying degrees. Dixie is still there and still different. But it is changing, and in some respects changing rapidly. Some of the qualities I have referred to are growing less distinctive and in some ways the South has become more like the rest of the United States; some would say indistinguishable. To travel through the Southern states is to explore a region whose people are conscious of differences and proud of some of them; but who are conscious also that economic growth and the relentless uniformity imposed by commerce and mass culture and communications are blurring and erasing some of the things that used to be part of the very fibre of the South.

Some people say, indeed, that the South, as an epoch, is finished.

It is tempting to talk of a new South, although people have been doing that from time to time for two or three generations. But, in the same way that there is always something new out of Africa, there is always something new out of Dixie; and I think that the changes of recent years enable us to draw a line under one chapter and consider a new one.

Every Southern child knows the names of the eleven states of the old Confederacy: Alabama, Arkansas, North Carolina, South Carolina, Florida, Georgia, Louisiana, Mississippi, Tennessee, Texas and Virginia. Today this is a region of fifty-five million people, racially and socially complex — black, brown and white — and shot through with contradictions.

The picture of the South as it came through novels, films and journalism always included magnolias, frame houses, porches with rocking-chairs and gregarious, patriotic people who loved their land and loved to tell stories and talk a lot, waited on by their black servants, and drawling to do justice to the language and to conserve strength on drowsy afternoons in the two months of the year when it is almost too hot to move. Against this backcloth the Southern novelists drew their pictures of passionate people and of the tensions in Southern society. There was racialism, cruelty, poverty, lynching, a propensity to murder, demagoguery and the long deep shadows of slavery and the Civil War.

Much of the scenery on the Dixie stage is still there, of course. Sweet magnolias are still as fragrant and glorious, there are still fried catfish for supper, there are still good manners and gentility, and lovely genteel Savannah, so civilized and proud, still has one of the highest murder rates in the whole country; and the rocking-chair remains a southern motif, even though television, the great leveller, has increasingly lured people off the back porch and into the parlour and

124

shut their chatting mouths. As for the players, well, they are as fiercely patriotic as ever, militaristic and moved by the sight of flags. But the play has changed radically and they have changed, too.

The guilt that stemmed from the two centuries of slavery and the deep and disturbed emotions that prevailed for many years after defeat in the Civil War have largely been eradicated. The wounds and bitterness caused in the struggles between blacks and recalcitrant whites in the civil rights campaigns of the 1950s and 1960s have to a considerable extent, although not entirely, healed. The changing fortunes of black people, the former peasantry, and the shifts in the black–white relationship are a large part of the fascinating transition of the South. Another part of it is economic growth. During the 1970s industrial production doubled; and the South is gowing faster than the North in economic terms. So the cities of the South are building more factories and skyscrapers and identical hotels. Hamburger places, ice cream parlours, all manner of American omnifoods, are supplementing, if not threatening, the catfish, corn bread, hush puppies and grits. The South, especially its urban spread, begins to look like the rest of America. And to sound like it, too. Television and radio people are breeding out their rich regional accents, dropping the distinctiveness, speaking faster and less intelligibly, and adopting the neutral tones that go with the required bland appearance and bland sound of a bland broadcasting system.

Some Southerners wring their hands to see a certain South fading. Some are genuinely concerned about the trimming of a culture, although one suspects that a few others are nostalgic for the days when the black man was kept under the heel by the South's cynical apartheid. Overall, the South has become more fully integrated with the rest of the United States and certainly more 'acceptable.' The election of Jimmy Carter, from Georgia, as President of the United States was part of this process of transition. Yankees and Rebels know each other better than ever before, thanks to commerce, television and the Interstate highways. Blacks and whites know each other a little better, too. In general, the South has broken free of the bonds of its history and is steadily shedding what remains of its once backward and tense social framework; though this takes time.

2

Grits, hominy grits, look like the semolina we used to get for school lunch. They are a kind of corn mash and lie there, glutinous, and sullen, upon the plate. Like chips in Britain they can be served with almost everything and, to a foreigner, or anyone from north of the Mason–Dixon line, are an acquired taste. One morning, while masticating this goo for breakfast in a store-cum-restaurant in a country town, I noticed a large sign reading: Steal From This Store At Your Own Risk. God Is Watching You.

There is little that is more Southern than grits and the invocation of God.

Organized religion is strong in the United States. More than half the people belong to a church. There are said to be more than a thousand religions catering to a wide spectrum of beliefs and interpretations, ranging from the orthodox to the extremely eccentric; so that the Almighty himself must be confused. In the South religion is especially strong and church-going deeply inculcated: no region of the country is more religious, and the warning to would-be shoplifters that God is watching is no doubt effective. Few people, having seen that, would risk being struck down by a heavenly thunderbolt. Throughout the South there are hundreds of little churches to be seen, with their spires and neat neon-signed car parks; and on Sundays you may see pink, white and yellow cars nuzzling around them, like piglets at a sow. Everywhere there is a profusion of hoardings and roadside signposts advertising the virtues of the faith, warning of the wages of sin, and pointing the way to a variety of churches.

> Smile, God Loves You.
> Jesus Still Makes House Calls.
> Sister Helen Spiritual Adviser Next Right.
> Prepare To Meet Thy God.
> A Family That Prays Together Stays Together.
> New Director Baptist Church.

Grand Old Gospel House.
Invest in God: Nine Per Cent Church Bonds.
Repent and Be Baptized Every One Of You.
Honk If You Love Jesus.

For black people in the South their churches, with their forms of worship and song tailored to the singular culture of the congregations, provided some relief from oppression and put some meaning into their lives. And the churches remain a powerful influence and undying force. For white people their churches provided in the post-Civil War period a comfort and reliable marker in a time of devastation and humiliation; and, no doubt, they were always able to provide comfort to enable white congregations to smooth over in their consciences their guilt about discrimination and the cruelties allied to it. There is in the white church in the South a long tradition of hypocrisy in this respect. Today the black and white churches in the South still tend to perform different roles: for many black people the church is much more an inspiration, an inculcator of pride and a community centre. It is a task that white churches do not perform to the same extent, because the need is not so great.

Nevertheless, in the South and throughout the United States, religion occupies the kind of place in society that it does not have in the largely post-Christian society of Britain. It may be that there are fears and empty spaces in the American way of life that do not exist to the same extent elsewhere. Certainly there is a craving for comfort and answers that is reflected in the growth of cults, religious and otherwise; and perhaps this growth says something about the suggestibility of many Americans. Many people go to church because they have a sincere and deep belief, others go out of habit, some because church attendance is a social custom; and others for political or business reasons. A lot of people go to church, not necessarily out of religious belief, but because church-going is part of being American. I imagine that the fact that Jimmy Carter was a professed 'born-again' Christian was part of his electoral appeal: it was part of his Americanness.

Religion for many Americans provides a wrap-around comfort. It is not meant to pose questions or be especially challenging and is shallow enough not to conflict with more deeply held views, or with selfishness, prejudice and hypocrisy.

Like food, religion in America is retailed in bright packages by super salesmen. The television and radio preachers, many of them raised in the Southern evangelical tradition, are among the sights of the land. On Sunday mornings they dominate the nation's airwaves. Smart in sales reps' suits these witchdoctors of electronica prance the stages in the cathedrals of schmaltz, sweating and quivering, bawling into their microphones, calling on huge audiences to be saved, to give themselves to God and their money to the churches. Organs play sugary tunes and choirs sing angelic ditties. The preachers reach frenzies of fervour of hernia proportions, and the audiences watch shiny-eyed. Such hot-gospellers are often the frontmen of busy, rich, huge businesses, for religion at this level is an industry. And television, through which they reach many millions in their regular Sunday spectaculars, is held to be the gift of God. Show business soul-gathering is something truly American.

3

Martin Luther King's widow, Coretta Scott King, is a dignified, rather formal, woman and striking in appearance. The pain of her loss can still be seen in her eyes and she evidently feels the weight of the responsibility she took on at her husband's death to ensure that his flame was kept bright. Her home in a suburb of Atlanta in Georgia is a centre for civil rights work and it is also a kind of museum. A large panelled basement room next to Dr King's study is covered with photographs and paintings illustrating chapters in Dr King's thirty-nine-year life, and with the trophies, awards and honorary degrees he won.

In Memphis, in April of 1968, a murderer stopped Martin Luther King, but not his revolution. Because of him and people like him, because of the movement of which he was a key part, the old institutionalized apartheid of the South has largely been ended and black people are increasingly taking a fuller part in the management and enjoyment of the society they share.

Mrs King reflected on the years since her husband's death. 'God knows, there is still a long road to tread,' she said to me, 'and there are still big wrongs to be righted. But we have to be optimistic and draw strength from our achievements. Martin had his dream, and parts of it have come true sooner than any of us dared to hope.'

After all, she said, it was not so long ago that black people suffered the oppression and indignities of the South's rigid caste system. Not only were they at the bottom of the economic heap; they also endured the constant hurts of segregation, the continuous insults and put-downs.

It wasn't so long ago. In the 1960s, a journalist told me, he was in a small racially mixed group travelling through the South and the black men in the party were refused service in restaurants. 'There were days when we got hungry on that trip. We had to find places where we could all be served together.'

For a century after the Civil War and the unlocking of the shackles of slavery, the black people of the South, and some parts of the North, too, lived under the humiliations and hardships imposed by the so-called Jim Crow laws. Jim Crow was a minstrel show character and the laws nicknamed after him formed a framework of apartheid and effectively prevented black people from enjoying the civil rights granted by the government after the war. Black people were prevented by law from free access to many buildings and institutions. Blacks and whites were segregated in schools, hotels, restaurants, churches, theatres, libraries, parks, lavatories and public seats. There were black and white telephone booths. The laws separated people on trains and buses and forbade blacks to serve on juries. As well as laws — and legal discrimination encouraged by the Supreme Court in one of its less glorious chapters — there were by-laws and social customs which made the black man chained. Black people could not use white swimming pools or try on clothes in shops that white people used, and they could not refresh themselves at drinking fountains reserved for whites. Some towns applied a curfew, ordering blacks out by sunset. A boy who looked at a white girl could be beaten up. Even in cold print, in a press which boasted of its freedom, there were separate columns for black births, marriages and deaths. As recently as 1956 a Southern newspaper doctored a photograph rather than allow a black face to appear alongside white faces: a picture of three white men and a black man was mutilated so that a white space appeared where the black man had been.

For many years after the Civil War segregation was reinforced by terror. The Ku Klux Klan roamed on its missions of suppression; and in many areas blacks received little help from those who were supposed to enforce the law. Indeed they were often as frightened of the enforcers as of the lawbreakers. And the bulk of the white public remained silent, either through apathy or fear. Between 1900 and 1931 there were one thousand eight hundred and eighty-six lynchings in the United States and one thousand five hundred and ninety-seven of them were in the eleven states of the old Confederacy.

And all the time other jabs of humiliation: as trains crossed the Mason–Dixon line and headed south black men left their seats and made their way to the blacks-only coaches.

Such a crude edifice of prejudice and cruelty was bound to crumble. The surprising thing is that it did not fracture sooner. Its rottenness was too much to withstand the anger that sprang from the aching hearts of oppressed people. When the hour came, there came the man also. The first blow at the institutionalized injustices of the South was landed by the Supreme Court in 1954 which overturned its colour bar ruling of fifty-eight years before and now declared that segregation in schools was unconstitutional. This struck at the core of the South's apartheid and set up ripples of fear and anger among whites. Some schools began to comply, but other authorities resisted. The stage was set for years of turmoil. It was not only that a way of life was under attack in the South; there was the question of the rights that Americans guard jealously. This time it was states' rights, the independence of the states, the right to run their affairs in the way they thought fit, without interference from central government: a constant theme of American politics. In the South, where people are especially defiant and resentful of encroachment, states' rights and the-right-to-do-as-I-damn-well-please, are sore issues. Southern corns are the most tender in America.

The second blow was struck in December of 1955 in Montgomery, Alabama. The city buses in Montgomery had segregated seating, whites at the front and blacks at the rear, and, if all the white seats were occupied a white person could go the black section and order a seat to be vacated. On a crowded bus one evening, Mrs Rosa Parks refused to give up her seat to a white man because she was tired. The driver called the police and she was arrested, and later fined ten dollars. Martin Luther King, who was then twenty-six, had just arrived in Montgomery as a Baptist minister. He helped to organize a boycott of the city's buses. Montgomery's black community, fifty thousand strong, took lifts, rode mules, but mainly walked for miles rather than ride the buses. And after eleven months the Supreme Court ruled that segregation on the buses was not constitutional. In the meantime the young Martin Luther King had been arrested and his home had been bombed. But the black people, some of them nervous and concerned at first, had found strength in daring together. They had dared to fight back; and Martin Luther King had tested and developed his philosophy and strategy of Gandhian non-violence to bring about change.

With his electrifying speeches he drew together the brave, the unsure and frightened, and showed them how they could challenge and at last overthrow the monstrous régime under which they lived. The fences of segregation began to come down. But there was resistance. There was rioting in Little Rock as the schools there were made to integrate.

Martin Luther King was arrested and imprisoned many times during the long civil rights campaign. In spite of the brutalities that his people suffered at the hands of certain police forces, town bosses, white extremists and terrorists, he never wavered from a strategy of non-violence. He never carried a gun. In a letter from the jail in Birmingham, Alabama, where he was imprisoned in 1963 he wrote: 'I stand in the middle of two opposing forces in the Negro community. One is a force of complacency made up of Negroes who, as a result of long years of oppression have been so completely drained of self-respect that they have adjusted to segregation, and, on the other hand, of a few Negroes in the middle class who, because of a degree of academic and economic security and because at points they profit from segregation, have unconsciously become insensitive to the problems of the masses. The other force is one of bitterness and hatred and comes perilously close to advocating violence. We need not follow the do-nothingism of the complacent or the hatred and despair of the black nationalist. I'm grateful to God that, through the Negro church, the dimension of non-violence entered our struggle. If this philosophy had not emerged I am convinced that by now many streets of the South would be flowing with blood ... ' A lot of people hated him and were afraid of him; and the FBI, under the autocratic J. Edgar Hoover, tapped his telephone and made efforts to discredit him on the grounds that he was subverting or otherwise endangering the stability of American society.

Great marches, prayer vigils and rallies, as well as King's oratory, marked the steady erosion of segregation. The greatest civil rights march of all, when a quarter of a million people walked through Washington in August 1963, was crowned by one of the finest of his speeches, delivered from the steps of the Lincoln Memorial, where Lincoln sits, stern and determined, looking out over the reflecting pool, to the Washington obelisk and the Capitol beyond. The speech lives still: to read it evokes at once the sight of Martin Luther King in impassioned flow. Much of what he said then remains true today, and he was talking a century after Lincoln had proclaimed emancipation of slaves. 'One hundred years later the Negro is still crippled by the manacles of segregation and the chains of discrimination, lives on a lonely island of poverty in the midst of a vast ocean of material prosperity ... '

'I have a dream,' he said. 'I have a dream that my four little children will one day live in a nation where they will not be judged by the colour of their skin but by the content of their character.'

The dream is still a long way from its realization. Discrimination and poverty which hallmark the existence of many blacks still provide the United States with one of its central torments and challenges. Black people have a shorter life expectancy than whites and their infant mortality rates are higher. So are their rates of separation and divorce. They suffer much more from high blood pressure. The tensions under which they live, the discrimination, unemployment and poorer housing, means that there is more mental illness among blacks than whites; and they find it difficult or impossible to afford medical treatment. Blacks live in worse housing conditions overall, have much higher unemployment and often can only find menial, low-paid and future-less jobs.

The races still live apart as a rule, the blacks in city centres and whites in the suburbs; and whites still make life hard for job-seeking blacks, taking on unqualified or poorly qualified whites in preference to trained blacks. Some trade unions, too, discriminate and make it difficult for young blacks to get into some jobs.

Black people struggled for years to dismantle the fences of segregation, but white American society still makes life harder for blacks. The discrimination is a little more subtle, the prejudice rather more covert. But in work, in education, in housing, in health, there are tens of thousands of black people who have to deal with a system in which, through a combination of hypocrisy, apathy, bigotry and fear, the scales are deliberately tipped against them.

I asked Mrs King about it. 'That's right. That's still a big battle. Civil rights were one thing, but Martin always said that black people needed economic rights as well. It's jobs we need for our people and our work now is towards full employment. It was the issue of economic rights that took Martin to Memphis where he was killed. Since his death I have worked to carry on his ideas. I've been an activist all my adult life and I won't stop.

'As I say, we still have a long road ahead. But when I look around I am amazed at some of the changes in our society. There are black mayors, legislators, and policemen, black people in jobs they could not have dreamt of getting a few years ago. There *is* progress. Those old signs we grew up with — Reserved for Whites, Whites Only — have been torn down. And those old racist politicians, you don't hear them now. They've been chased away, or they've shut up, or they've changed the way they think ... '

She no doubt had in mind George Wallace, elected governor of Alabama in 1962, who said in his inaugural speech: 'Segregation now. Segregation tomorrow. Segregation forever.' But Mr Wallace later changed his tune, and so did other segregationists when they saw how the tide was turning.

'And even policemen,' Mrs King said, 'have learnt to be polite.'

Discrimination, of course, is by no means a Southern phenomenon. 'It was always the South that had a bad name for prejudice,' Mrs King reflected, 'but events have shown that there is just as much in the North. I think racial tension has subsided, but attitudes do not change overnight and there is still discrimination.'

A lot of Southerners I met were swift to say that cities in the North had been tried and found wanting when it came to race relations. There is, ironically, a kind of Southern pride in the way the Dixie states buckled down and integrated.

In Memphis, at the headquarters of the Cotton Council of America, I was told: 'We think the South has the best race relationships of any part of the United States, and many younger blacks are returning from the North to the South because opportunities for work are improving all the time and because whites and blacks get along better now. After all, we have been together a long time in the South, and we've got to know each other.'

I thought some Southerners were rather smug about it. 'All those northern liberals and students, holier than thou, telling us what to do. Seems they couldn't get their own house in order ... '

Southerners forget that many of them resisted integration, that the government had to send soldiers to help children go to school when whites were beside themselves with hysterical rage, that the South would hardly have ended its degraded régime had it not been obliged to do so by the civil rights movement and the government.

Nevertheless some states fairly quickly disposed of the paraphernalia of segregation; and there are many black people, as Martin Luther King's widow said, who believe that race relations in the South are better now than in the North. Walter Walker, black president of Le Moyne Owen college in Memphis, told me that he thought blacks and whites got on relatively better in the South because they had a greater experience of each other. 'I've lived in the North, in Chicago. I would often go for three or four days without seeing a white person, and that is part of the trouble. People don't get familiar with each other, so there's suspicion and nervousness.

'Actually, I don't think racism is the overriding problem. I think racism can work itself out in time. Things do improve gradually. There are two blacks on the Chamber of Commerce board in Memphis, unthinkable a few years ago. I cannot think of a single civil rights measure that we need now. Those battles have been fought, though the government is not fulfilling promises on civil rights. Its attitude is still one of benign neglect. The blacks' major difficulty is lack of money. There seems to be no solution in law for economic problems but somehow we have to get jobs for black people. Only jobs, and the money and the dignity that go with them, will give blacks a truly equal place in society.'

4

One of the influences in the raising of black consciousness and pride in recent years is said to be *Roots*, the book that Alex Haley took twelve years to write. 'It became an obsession with me, to trace my family history, and as the book grew I could see that it was developing into the story of my people,' he said when I met him near Los Angeles. 'I did not begin with a lofty purpose, but I can see that *Roots* has given people a history and a pride. It has shown black people how they fit into America and how they helped to build it. I think it has enabled white people to understand the black man better. The book came out at just the right time. In the social climate of the United States ten or fifteen years ago, with all the demonstrations and turmoil, it would have been viewed as an inflammatory book and would have run into trouble. Perhaps in a way it's been a kind of balm. I get a lot of letters from blacks and from whites telling me it has stimulated their interest in history, in the story of America. Some people wanted me to be a kind of black leader because of *Roots*, but I could never be that. I'm a writer who has told a story. At the same time I feel a sense of responsibility to black people and I have been determined never to let them down. Sure it's a pleasure to have written the number one book in the world, but a greater pleasure to know it was written by a black man.'

14
MR KLAN

Opinions founded on prejudice are always
sustained with the greatest violence.
Lord Jeffery

David Duke, eyes like Fox's Glacier Mints, came into the room
all of an important bustle and it was evident almost at once that
taciturnity was not his strong suit. He was neat, alert, serious,
unsmiling and let his words flow as water from a cistern. He
had at his elbow a fat, red-eyed and uncouth young man who
said nothing and maintained an expression of unrelieved
sullenness. As the so-called 'grand wizard' and national
director of one of the factions of the Ku Klux Klan Mr Duke
had come to a hotel room in New Orleans to talk with some
visiting reporters about the Ku Klux Klan which, although
small, remains an object of interest. One of the reporters was
black and wore a teeshirt decorated with a pair of bright red
lips and the inscription *Kiss Me I'm Black*. Mr Duke's pale eyes
changed from mint to flint. He settled into a chair, his smart
light suit, fair hair, toothbrush moustache and youthful
appearance thrown into more agreeable relief by the sloppy
demeanour of his unpleasant-looking fat friend. Mr Duke
called for questions, but answered none of them. Rather, he
used them as points to switch himself on to well-used tracks of
talk and which always switched him back again to his main
themes. If there were a persistent questioner he shook him off,
as he might a fly, and he rattled tediously on through his
tunnels of gloom and bigotry and distortion.

His admirers always describe him as an articulate man; and

his publicity material quotes people, including television inter-viewers, who have remarked on this quality. They may, however, have mistaken loquaciousness for articulateness. Mr Duke can talk all right. He is a lexicographical cataract. The difficulty is in keeping him to the point and getting him to stop. On this occasion he was unwilling, perhaps unable, to debate, to respond either cogently or concisely. What was irritating about him was not so much his tirade against Jews and black people, gobbets of well-worn Nazism, but his lack of manners in his determination not to pause, and the way he used the event to buff his ego.

The Ku Klux Klan is one of the pieces of the stereotype collage of America that everybody knows. Along with cow-boys and Indians, hamburgers, skyscrapers, the drawl, Coca Cola and big cars, the Ku Klux Klan, its bogey-man robes and its fiery crosses, has its own dark small corner in the thumbnail sketch of the United States.

It is unfair and distorted, but such images usually are. And if the Klan gets attention it is because of its violent past, its fancy dress, its part in the history of race relations, its willingness to say aloud what some people think privately and perhaps guiltily; and because extremism and bizarrerie are objects of curiosity and fit one of the definitions of news. It also gives a shivering glimpse of evil.

The branches of the Ku Klux Klan are small. Leaders of them rarely discuss the size of membership because they are embarrassed by the paucity of their numbers. They prefer to claim that they have hundreds of thousands of adherents, even millions, and that they are presiding over a resurgence. The Federal Bureau of Investigation, whose agents keep a watch on the Klan, has details of more than twelve Ku Klux Klan branches and thinks that there are fewer than two thousand of what it calls 'hard core' activists, adding that there are no doubt some thousands of people of more watery allegiance. The Anti-Defamation League, a New York-based Jewish organization, which also keeps tabs on the Ku Klux Klan and other extremist groups, thinks there are more Klan members than the FBI estimates, but that the Klan is, nevertheless, quite small. The League says that the Ku Klux Klan in its present form is 'a good thing for us because it is tiny and reveals the sickness from which it springs. It serves too, as a warning signal, reminding people of what can happen if bigotry takes root. And it can still make trouble locally, exacerbating community issues such as the bussing of children to school.'

The Ku Klux Klan is a pustule on the American body politic and seems to swell at times of economic recession and social turmoil.

The original Klan existed for only three or four years. It was founded after the Civil War by former Confederate soldiers appalled at seeing their world turned upside-down in the immediate post-war reconstruction which gave the blacks — their former serfs — freedom and the right to hold public office. They established an organization they called the Kuklos, the Greek word for circle which was fashioned eventually into Ku Klux; and they started intimidating black voters. Their weapons of terror were blazing crosses, white robes and torchlight rides into the depths of the night. The tougher and less superstitious blacks who would not be cowed by these methods were set upon by bigot brigades and were beaten up, tarred and feathered or lynched. The violence sickened many members of the Klan and, with the government taking steps to outlaw the organization, it was disbanded.

The white community, however, resorted to other devices to keep the blacks down; segregation, unjust laws and pressure which persisted into the 1960s. In 1915, more than forty years after disbandment, a second Klan was founded by an ex-minister of religion who widened its appeal of prejudice. The new Klan was not only white supremacist, but anti-semitic, anti-Catholic, anti-birth control, and anti-pacifism. At a time of new fears and exploitable ignorance its appeals to the white multi-chauvinism that has always been a stream in American society and politics were irresistible to many.

Blacks were moving into Northern cities and immigration was presented as a threat to the American nation. The whites in the South expressed their fear in a wave of beatings, arson and lynchings; and posed for photographs, grinning, silly and gawping beneath the swinging bodies of their hapless victims. By the middle of the 1920s the Klan reached a peak membership of between four and five million and was deeply involved in terrorism. There was a kind of hysteria blowing in some parts of the South and demagogues throve. (A generation later a similar wind blew again in America, this time an anti-Communist hysteria which fuelled the McCarthy era of witch-hunts and underpinned the chillingly named UnAmerican Activities Committee.)

The flaring of the Klan in the 1920s was relatively brief, though bloody. Press disclosures of terrorism and murder, and of corruption in the Klan, led to a sudden and large-scale apostasy among members and within a few years only a frag-mented remnant remained.

Klanism still lurked, though. And it reared itself again when the black people began their civil rights campaigning in the 1950s and white people saw that their apartheid systems might be dismantled. Again, the Ku Klux Klan was involved in violence, in beatings and killings.

The modern Ku Klux Klan attempts to win for itself a certain respectability by apparently forswearing violence. It still holds cross burnings and its members wear their sinister white robes and hoods and get their pictures in the papers. But at least one Klan group does not profess non-violence. Its members come to meetings with sub-machine guns and sawn-off shotguns; and its leaders observe tersely: 'These guns are not for rabbit hunting. They are to waste people.'

The stock-in-trade of the Ku Klux Klan is a perverted and paranoid prejudice masquerading as patriotism; and, although the Klan today claims a growing support among the better educated, its appeal is essentially to the disgruntled and resentful at the lower end of the social and intellectual scale. To the suggestible it offers easy solutions and readily identified scapegoats, the blacks, Jews, liberals and communists, so that it is a movement entirely without responsibility.

David Duke's faction of the Ku Klux Klan has a seedy Patriot Book Store, with meshed windows, in a suburb of New Orleans, where the Klan sells books like *The Hitler We Loved And Why*, and *The Jews and Their Lies*. It also sells confe-derate flags ('no longer a sectional emblem, now a symbol of the white race') and White Power tee-shirts. A white Klan robe, in permanent press polyester and cotton, retails for twenty-eight dollars.

Members of some Ku Klux Klan factions are against the

adding of fluoride to drinking water, among other things. Rather more seriously, they are strongly in favour of gun-toting and are vehemently opposed to gun control. At rallies they sometimes raffle a rifle, and their publications offer three-dollar booklets like *Boobytraps, Incendiaries* and *The Improvised Munitions Handbook*.

Voluble Mr Duke was rattling on at his visitors, seemingly unstoppable. His technique is to hose his listeners with words and irrigate their fears with the commonplaces of prejudice.

But here his listeners were tired of him and examining their nails and their watches. He had no new ideas to relate. 'We are in a war,' he said. 'White people in this country are the oppressed minority. Jews control broadcasting and publishing and there should be quotas for them in these fields. Meanwhile the higher birthrate of the black man means that whites will be swamped. We now have Klan border patrols to report Mexicans getting into the country illegally. We are doing our duty as Americans. We are certainly not the lunatic fringe. Sure, I know all about *Roots*, I know it's a big seller. But I call it a slap in the face for white people. We believe people should be allowed to pursue their own cultures. We believe in brotherhood among people.'

It was such a relief when the grand wizard was forced by the blessed onset of the lunch hour to end his rhetoric. It was as if a record had been switched off. He gathered up his notes and his dumb, sullen, henchman and strode off to pursue brotherhood among people. It was so peaceful when he had gone.

15
THE MULE AND I

To stand upon the edge of this stupendous gorge is to enjoy in a moment compensation for years of uneventful life.

John L. Stoddard

The mule regarded me evenly and I looked into his eyes in the hope of establishing rapport. None was established. This was my first meeting with the all-American jackass, unsung burden-beast of exploration and settlement. There was not much to say about this individual. His name was Holy Smoke. He was brown and long-eared and rather dusty, with an uncombed look. He was somewhat larger than I had expected, much more horse than ass, a substantial animal, and was of unenthusiastic mien: had he been a man he would have been leaning, bored and unkempt, against a wall with a cigarette on his lip edge and a lump of gum in his mouth. His feet were large and round, like joints of Sunday-roast sirloin. To these, to the skill and instinct with which he would make his steps, I was entrusting my life.

I looked at him, therefore, in an effort to assess his attitude. Did he feel resentful because, as Robert Ingersoll, the American lawyer, said: 'a mule has neither pride of ancestry nor hope of posterity.' Can mules become depressed? Would this be the journey in which he would decide to end it all and throw himself and rider into the greatest abyss on the planet? Was he waiting to avenge some real or imagined slight, some unwarranted kick or beating? His eyes told me nothing. They had in them the expression that old lift attendants have, a compound of patience and ennui. I rubbed my hand against his neck in a comradely you-and-me-together-old-pal gesture, but he was unimpressed. There seemed to be no way of forging the man-and-his-mount liaison I had read about, no way of being Roy Rogers to his Trigger.

A tough and weathered-looking man in a western hat appeared at my shoulder and gave me a switch of whippy sapling. 'This one,' he said, jerking his head towards my allotted steed, 'is a lazy son of a bitch. So use this on him good and hard.' I looked into the mule's face. He'd heard all right. I fancied that his eyes narrowed and I wished the man had not talked so loudly.

I put my luggage, a toothbrush and a razor and comb, into one of the small canvas saddlebags slung behind the worn and shiny saddle and, grasping the saddle horn, swung myself aboard. The leatherwork creaked as I slotted in. There were nine of us in the group and our guide was a man called Bud who was thin and tough and tanned; wiry and confident and, you could tell, with a sense of humour. He used words economically, as if they were in short supply. Like the other man who was checking bridles and buckles, he wore a well-used light-grey hat. And, as with so many men in the American west, the hat was part of his persona, as if it had been fastened on to his head in young manhood and had slowly taken root, so that no sudden gust of wind would ever lift it. Indeed, I can remember only one or two instances when I saw a hatted rural westerner remove his Stetson, and it was rather like the surprise you get when you see a person who is habitually spectacled remove his glasses.

Once, in Texas, I saw a big cowboy raise his hat to draw his hand across his sweating brow, and there was a deep groove in his forehead, so that I was put in mind of the skull-shaping practices of certain peoples. And without his hat for a second or two the man looked utterly different, almost vulnerable. In the west, the hats are part of masculinity and a child might grow up believing that men are men because they are hatted. The hats are often worn indoors as well as out, I noticed, and I wondered if they were also worn in the bath and in bed.

Bud, looking out from beneath the brim moulded to his head, tightened saddle cinches around the mules' bellies and adjusted stirrup straps. Then he slipped swiftly, as a hand into

142

a glove, into his own saddle and led us out of the corral and over the southern rim of the Grand Canyon of the Colorado, in north-west Arizona. Far below in the mile deep canyon ran the swirling caramel river, still working as mighty adze, auger and plane on its immense and fabulous sculpture.

It was a hot early morning in April. The sky was bright blue with a few puffs of cumulus, the air clear and the canyon fresh. The mules plodded and farted steadily in Indian file along the steep stony track winding its corkscrew way downwards. And I soon saw now how the mules tormented their human burdens.

Although the tracks were narrow, with no room for one mule to pass another, the mules did not stay as close as possible to the canyon wall. Rather, they walked as close as possible to the friable edge of the track as if playing a grisly game of chicken. Thus each rider had the impression of being on a tightrope, each man his own Blondin. And on muleback to boot. Glancing down I could see my right foot apparently suspended over a long and terrifying drop as the mule persisted in his hair-raising brinkmanship. My imagination wandered over the possibilities of mule coronaries, saddle-cinch failure, and sudden track subsidence. The tops of conifers were far below, and so were slabs of red and yellow rock, beautiful and bone-breakingly terminal. The instinct was to lean inwards as a counter-balance, and to try to steer the flatulent hybrid who now had charge of my life away from the brink. But he obstinately trod his tightrope, no doubt having a grim and mulish chuckle to himself.

After a while, on a slightly wider part of the track, Bud called a halt and the mules obediently slowed and half-turned, facing out over the canyon and moving to the daredevilest edge of the precipice: another inch and each of us would have been riding Pegasus. Through their waggling ears we had a heart-knocking view of the chasm and eternity. Bud said: 'Don't lean inwards. Sit up straight and trust the mules. They've been doing this all their lives, and they know best. And keep up. It's dangerous to get behind. If you've gotta beat them to keep up, beat them. It's not cruel, it's for your own safety and for theirs. And no one, whatever happens, gets off his mule. It's dumb and it's dangerous. Stay on. Keep up. Let's go.'

We stepped back on to the serpentine tightrope, our lives in their feet. I imagine that, for a parachutist, the first dry-throated half-second of his leap is as a birth: however much he wishes to do so, he may not return to the womb of the plane. In the same way, by the time I had appreciated the size of the enterprise I was embarked upon, it was too late for reconsideration. Thus I felt that flush of exhilaration and freedom that comes with taking an irrevocable step and a risk. After a while I grew used to being on the back of an animal which stubbornly insisted on being a mulish Harold Lloyd and walking the parapet of a skyscraper. Heights make my palms perspire and give a little kick in the stomach. But after a few minutes I began to feel that the mule knew what he was doing and my palms began to dry.

The journey by mule to the bottom of the Grand Canyon takes about six hours, a descent of five thousand feet. We travelled by way of the Bright Angel Trail, so that we had hours to marvel at the sights of the Upper Granite Gorge and the vast cathedrals of rock named in awe: Wotan's Throne, Brahma Temple, the Tower of Ra, the Tower of Set and Point Sublime. People have been making this journey for years and, as far as I know, no mule has ever cast his rider into the Colorado. Any close exploration beneath the canyon rim is bound to be physically exacting. Of course, you may fly, in a small aeroplane or helicopter, and I am told that it is a marvellous experience. But —and maybe I have a puritan streak lurking — there is much to be said for sweating for the pleasure of the canyon, so that its sheer might and titanic beauty are appreciated not through the eyes only, but through the lungs and muscles and nerves; and, intrepid mule riders reflect ruefully later, the backside.

I remember a woman telling me, some years ago, that scenery of any kind bored her, that she found it curious that the folds, lumps, cracks and pits in the earth's skin inspired wonder and led to sentimental exalting. But even she (soulless I thought her) would surely have regarded, with a caught breath and a child's sense of wonder, the astonishing canyon cut by the cheesewire Colorado over millions of years. Invariably it brings on chronic attacks of adjectival gluttony: it is not simply a stupendous view, but vistas heaped upon panoramas. It is an episode, an aesthetic as well as physical experience. The

144

canyon is magnificently dangerous and forbidding, so that it is easy to understand why a visiting nineteenth-century parson should write of it: 'Horror! Tragedy! Silence! Death! Chaos! There is the awful canyon in five words ... the delirium of nature.'

The canyon is two hundred and seventeen miles long and is, indeed, a collection of canyons. Apart from its enormous size and the ruggedness and grandeur of rock formations, its colouring is an endless entertainment, inspiration and solace. It is a chameleon of a canyon. The swiftly changing values of the light sweep it constantly with fresh colour washes. When I arrived at the southern rim, having driven up from Flagstaff, the sun was low and the canyon was beginning to shut down for the night: pillars and buttes blazed like a fire of Welsh anthracite, but the shadows were deep and deepening; dark slatey blues, umbers and dark ochres, mauves and inky purples.

Now, on this crystal morning, on the anguine Bright Angel Trail, the canyon colours were as fresh as they are in the newly severed halves of a watermelon. Pink on pink, on brown on red on orange on buff, bright as the stripes on cricket club ties, and it changed by the minute; pink blush growing to red flush and back again as the sun climbed and the clouds trailed skidding shadows.

The sun was hot on bare forearms and faces and the mules' hooves were throwing up dust to grit our teeth as we came through some scrub about three thousand feet beneath the canyon rim and into the cool shaded green oasis called Indian Garden. The mules were hitched to a rail and we walked stiffly to the tall parasol of the cottonwood trees and drank spring water and ate a sandwich. My knees felt like rusted hinges and I now realized why only fit people weighing under fourteen stone are permitted to take the mule trek. Indian Garden, a pretty place, gratefully reached, is a sour footnote in the canyon's history. It was once the home of Havasupai Indians who were evicted because their presence there did not suit the white man's plans. The canyon was designated a national monument in 1908 and a national park eleven years later.

Wishing that my knees could be oiled, I mounted up and put the mule into gear. We rode past the rushing waters of Garden Creek and came at last to the fearsome Devil's Corkscrew which is guaranteed to expose any latent acrophobia. The track was thin, steep and tortuous, a test of mule and coward; and tantalizing because at the end of every hairpin bend we expected to find relief and an easy ride, only to see in front of us what seemed to be a rugged helterskelter.

But, at last, even the corkscrew ended. The mules splashed across a fast stream and we rode down Pipe Creek before turning east to ride the trail cut in the cliff above the surging, urgent Colorado. Still the mules tested our nerves, keeping close to the edge so that we could see our left feet sticking out into the air, with the hungry, galloping river a hundred or two hundred feet below; and no safety net. Quite suddenly, we entered a cool tunnel bored into the rock and emerged on the Kaibab Bridge, a single-file span five feet wide and four hundred and forty feet long slung across the gorge. We clattered across and turned north up Bright Angel Creek. And soon we found the tall cottonwood trees, the log cabins, the corral and the big wooden dining hall of Phantom Ranch, south of Phantom Canyon. We were covered with a brown-red dust and our mouths were so dry that we felt, as Davy Crockett expressed it, that we could spit cotton. We drank cool water from a ladle and went to our quarters, simple cabins with bunks that are repose for the mule-worn and stiff-kneed. A gong sounded tinnily from the dining hall and we fell upon steaks that seemed then, and in retrospect, among the great steaks of all time. The best thing to do after that was to sit and look at the stars. But not for long. On one hand there was total fatigue, and, on the other, the prospect of the dawn start next day and the magnificent return journey to the south rim.

I was fortunate to explore this fragment of the canyon at a time of the year when the human traffic there was light. As with other natural temples of grandeur and freedom and wilderness, in North America and many other parts of the world, the Grand Canyon is under heavy pressure from its pilgrims' feet. The people who lived here from prehistoric times, whose grain jars, simple tools and rock paintings are still being discovered, hardly marked it. And for four hundred years after Spaniards saw it on one of their expeditions, the canyon was big enough to cope with the trickle, then the flow, of white men. Today, however, the greatest difficulty of the national park authorities is to cope with the crowds. In 1903, President Theodore Roosevelt visited the canyon and urged people to do nothing to mar its grandeur. 'Leave it as it is,' he said. 'You cannot improve on it. Keep it for your children, your children's children, and for all who come after you as the one great sight which every American should see … '

Many Americans agree with him. In the last part of the 1960s two million people went to the canyon every year and now three million go. At peak times in the summer the approach roads on the south rim are jammed with cars and the hotels, restaurants and souvenir shops are packed. On a summer's day there might be more than a thousand people walking the Bright Angel Trail, each footstep wearing the trail a fraction more. In accordance with canyon etiquette the hikers stand still as the mules pass them by, and the mules' hooves also do their bit of damage to the trail. I was reminded that, in north Wales, there is similar concern that the paths of Snowdon are being worn out, and that walkers and climbers are urged to carry a stone with them when they ascend, to help repair the damaged parts.

In an effort to protect the canyon, and its visitors, the national park authorities have already imposed limits on the number of campers entering the canyon at popular times. They have cut down on the numbers of people who can go on the exciting, bouncing boat trips along the river; and there is a strong belief that motor boats should be banned from the river. As these boats earn more than two million pounds a year the operators are naturally opposed to a ban. This sort of argument is being heard increasingly in America's wilderness areas. There are many walkers and campers who want undisturbed peace, the total protection of the ecology, nature in the raw, and engines outlawed. The men who run the helicopter and aeroplane trips that disturb the walkers' peace say: 'Why the hell shouldn't people see the canyon in any way they wish — and, anyway, helicopters don't wear out the trails.' And the motor boat operators say that the national park belongs to all the people, not just to the pedestrian élitists.

The national park authorities may have to introduce overall quotas to control the number of daily visitors, so that, at popular times, the canyon could be closed by noon. They would like to move most of the ugly commercial developments on the south rim back a few miles, and run a shuttle service from car parks to the rim. There is talk of strengthening some of the heavily used trails with hard-wearing plastic rock that mimics the real thing. Clearly, as the pressure grows the canyon keepers will have to strike their balances and fight fierce battles to do so.

Meanwhile, on a day in early spring, the canyon is still uncrowded, wild and challenging, and leaves no room in the imagination and the senses for anything else. Stiff and dusty I dismounted at last from the sweating old soldier of a mule who had wound his way again up the Bright Angel tightrope. There may be plastic rocks one day, but never plastic mules. Bud came up and, using the mule's rump as a desk, wrote his signature on a certificate authenticating the two-day journey. 'Come again one day,' he said. 'Thanks,' I said. 'You bet,' he said.

16
UNCLE SAM'S SOMBRERO

Keep in the front of your heads all the time, dear ladies, first that you are the descendants of immigrants.

Franklin D. Roosevelt

In the cool shadows inside the old white stone Alamo mission in San Antonio stands the Red Dragon Flag of Wales. It is a memorial to two Welshmen, William Lewis and Lewis Johnson, whose fates drew them to death in the tumult of the Alamo at the side of American heroes like Davy Crockett, William Travis and Jim Bowie. The flags of England and Scotland and Ireland are there, too, representing the sprinkling of men from those countries who found themselves in the dry-throated dawn of March 6, 1836, loading their muskets as a great army of Mexicans bore down on them. All the one hundred and eighty-eight Alamo defenders perished that day in the most famous and desperate battle of the Texan war of independence. The hoarse cry of 'Remember the Alamo!' helped to stoke up emotions and pump adrenalin in a battle forty-six days later in which Texans defeated the Mexican army. The victors proclaimed the republic of Texas; and this, ten years later, joined the United States.

The Alamo is much smaller than anyone who has watched John Wayne defending it would imagine. It is no larger than a little village church in England and its size and vulnerability put the plight and courage of the defenders into a better perspective. With its plaques and relics and heroic cenotaph it is a national shrine. Texans have great pride in it and insist that we still 'Remember the Alamo'; though they themselves forgot it to the extent that part of it was nearly sold as a site for a hotel, and would no doubt today be the Alamo Hilton had not a Texan lady with a sense of history stepped in, bought it, and beaten the businessmen.

Although presented today as unblemished heroes, whose altruism and love of freedom led them to die for Texas, the defenders of the Alamo were the usual job lot of men you would have expected to find in those unordered times on a new frontier. Some represented settlers who resented Mexican rule of the Texan province; some were agitators who wanted to kick the Mexicans out and bring Texas into the union for the greater glory of the United States; some were adventurers, men with few ties who did not mind a fight.

As for their leaders, William Travis was under a cloud, in virtual exile having killed a man; James Bowie, whose name is associated with the large hunting knife he popularized, was a former slave trader, forger and robber; and Davy Crockett, frontiersman and congressman, had marched off to Texas with some fellow Tennesseans in a bitter mood after political disappointment.

The war of which they were part may have wrested Texas from Mexico. It did not however take it away from Mexicans. Texas, like other regions of the south-west, is a sponge state which has been steadily soaking up migrant Mexicans. In the past few years America has begun to realize that in its south-west there is growing a bilingual section of the nation that is of increasing importance and influence. For the United States the rapid expansion of this sub-group, the fastest growing minority, poses one of the great social, economic and political challenges of the late twentieth century. The flavour of the south-west is changing; it is a unique mixture of Spanish and English cultures, of Mexican and American outlooks. I wonder what Crockett and Co. would have made of this burgeoning Mexamerica.

San Antonio, lush, sub-tropical, gracious, with its amiable river winding lazily through its heart, is the tenth largest city in the country, and more than half its people are Mexican. It has the sort of atmosphere that Europeans like — unfrenetic and more easy-going than most American cities; and it owes much to the colour and graces that Mexicans have brought to it, their manners, cuisine and customs, their dress, architecture and, of course, their language.

In other centres Mexicans are rooting and flowering. Sprawling Los Angeles has more than one and a half million people of Mexican blood, so that it is second only to Mexico City as a concentration of Mexicans. Some parts of southern Texas, along the valley of the Rio Grande, have a population more than nine-tenths Mexican. And more Mexicans arrive every day.

In Los Angeles Mexican Americans outnumber black and white children in the schools. For many people, teachers, policemen and public officials, the ability to speak Spanish is becoming essential. Los Angeles police cadets take a six-month course in Spanish, and education authorities are trying to teach more Spanish in some areas, a difficult task in a country where the learning of foreign languages is little more than a fringe activity.

The Mexican threads in the American cloth are becoming brighter. Mexican restaurants and fast-food stalls are spreading. Among the Irish names of Roman Catholic priests there is an increasing number of Spanish names. Record shops are carrying more Spanish-language pop songs. In cities and towns where there is a strong Mexican element advertisements are often in Spanish. So are public signs, official directions and instructions. There are nearly forty Spanish-language radio stations in Texas, and nearly forty throughout California, New Mexico and Arizona; and Spanish-language television channels operate from San Antonio and Los Angeles.

The Spanish-speaking people of the United States, from Mexico, Cuba and Puerto Rico, the United States' island possession in the Caribbean, number twelve million, according to the census of 1978. But this count does not include an estimated seven or eight million illegal immigrants. It is reckoned that during the 1980s the numbers of Hispanics will outnumber black people, who make up about an eighth of the American population.

Hispanics are beginning to feel the muscle that great numbers build. The Mexican Americans, who call themselves Chicanos, a corruption of Mexicano, are by far the largest group and want a fatter slice of the American pie. There are more than seven million of them officially accounted for; and there are millions more who crossed the border illegally in search of a better life. As the leading minority in the south-west Chicanos are increasingly making their presence felt, socially and politically.

Many Anglo-Americans watch this minority-on-the-move with some disquiet. For them the Mexicans — Spanish-speaking, Catholic, brown, sensuous, different in many ways — seem to offer a threat to their jobs, their way of life and to their comfort in a comfortable land. It is by no means a new story in the United States where there has always been a strain of anti-alienism and the hypocrisy that goes with it. But prejudice and tension are growing.

Like people anywhere, many white Americans are concerned about changes in their society brought about by immigration. Thus there is much attention directed to the border between the United States and Mexico which is nearly two thousand miles long. It is a very leaky border. Mexicans have crossed it illegally in their hundreds of thousands. They have walked, driven and waded and swum across — hence their nickname of wetbacks. They have hidden in the false bottoms of vans and lorries and half suffocated in the boots of cars. They have been caught in their droves, dumped back in Mexico, and have picked themselves up and started all over again.

The wetback is an intractable problem for the United States. His success in evading the border patrol causes concern or outrage, depending on the point of view, and his arrival in the towns and cities causes enormous and complicated social difficulties. There is a lot of growling about illegal aliens, and rednecks like the Ku Klux Klan sometimes go off and do what they conceive as their patriotic duty, and patrol the border themselves. The question of illegal immigration is a sensitive one in the relationship between the United States and Mexico, and has indeed, chilled the soup when president has met president.

The American outlook is ambiguous. The truth is that the United States imports a working class to do jobs that most Americans will not do. Americans do not like to admit it, any more than they like to admit they have an imperialist history. But migrant labour is encouraged to come to the United States to pick crops and do menial work, often for wages and in conditions that most Americans would find contemptible. Migrants, legal or wetback, can have a very hard time of it in the United States. But still they come. For America, as it has always been, is still a promised land.

2

The wetback trail is a kind of safety valve. Mexico's greatest problem is a population explosion which casts a deep shadow over a country working hard to develop its resources, whose prospects for growth based on oil and other natural wealth are excellent. The growth of population is phenomenal and a source of anxiety. Even optimists are not certain that efforts to slow the rate of growth have begun in time to prevent turmoil.

At the beginning of the twentieth century the population of Mexico was fifteen million. In 1940 it was twenty million and now it is more than sixty-five million. The birth rate is three times that of the United States and three-quarters of Mexicans are under the age of twenty-two. By the end of this century the population will be at least one hundred million. Such growth is creating huge pressures for a country that in terms of modern industrial and economic development is still a young one. Mexico City already has about fourteen million people, making it the largest city in the world; and its population is swelled by the people from the countryside who save the one-way fare to the capital and arrive at the station at the rate of one thousand every day. It seems that nothing can stop Mexico City growing to a megatropolis of twenty-five million, living in daunting congestion.

The government now encourages birth control. But until the early 1970s Mexico's policies and Mexican attitudes encouraged an increase in population. Mexico is not only a Catholic country but also one where *machismo* is a great force: a man's virility is measured by the size of his family. Moreover, Mexicans have long been taught that large parts of their country are depopulated. 'We wonder if the measures we are taking to slow the rate of population growth are being taken soon enough,' a Mexican lawyer said to me. 'We have a race against time. We are finding the wealth we need to finance our progress, but unless we take care our difficulties will grow too monstrous to conquer.'

Agrarian reform in Mexico has failed to meet the expectations of many of the people, simply because there are too many people. Large tracts of Mexico are unsuitable for agriculture, and there is not enough land to go round. The prospects are of unemployment and under-employment, a continuing and increasing drift from the land. The young educated people will want jobs. Young men will consider the prospects in their own country, and will compare these with what the United States has to offer. By comparison the United States is a land of plenty, of high wages and opportunity. So, in increasing numbers, men and women travel the wetback trail.

Commander Lou Reiter, of the Los Angeles police, said: 'You just can't blame them. A Mexican who comes to the United States can earn in one year what it would take him ten years to earn in his own country. Even in a menial job. Mexico simply hasn't industrialized and developed enough to absorb its unemployed. There are huge numbers of people out of work. It is estimated that these illegal aliens, or undocumented aliens as we call them, earn more than ten billion dollars a year, and this is four per cent of Mexico's gross national product.'

Commander Reiter sees a lot of the trouble that the wetbacks can get into. He is sympathetic. He knows what drives men to risk the humiliation and the hardship and danger that may lie in store for them when, often with families to feed, they make a break for it and strike out for a better life. He knows that the United States is not committed wholeheartedly to stopping immigration, and that the wetbacks play a part in the economy. Mexicans till the fields and pick the crops in many parts of the United States. Farmers in the Rio Grande valley of Texas once took part in an official drive against illegal immigrants, organized by the Immigration Service, but could not get people to do their crop picking. In the end the Immigration Service had to allow them to do what they had always done, and import labour from south of the border.

No one knows how many Mexicans have entered illegally. Estimates range from a few million to fifteen million. About one million people are apprehended by the Immigration Service every year and are deported. On an eighteen-mile stretch of the border in California the authorities arrest about thirty thousand every month, and estimate that another sixty thousand actually wriggle through the net.

It is a kind of sad and desperate game and there are a lot of losers. Apart from those who cross the Rio Grande and steal in by night, there are others who pay a 'coyote', a smuggler, to get them across. It can cost a few hundred dollars for an uncomfortable and scary ride hidden in the boot of a car or in the back of a lorry. Once inside the United States a man makes for the districts where he has friends and relatives, and at least people who speak his own language. He goes to the *barrio* in Los Angeles, or San Antonio, or some other town, and begins to dig himself in. For a while he will live in squalor and will be vulnerable to those who prey on those who live in the wetback limbo.

Commander Reiter said: 'Mexico doesn't want the illegal aliens back and we have to make the effort to patrol the border and send back those who come in undocumented. The problem for us is that undocumented aliens make a demand on the police service which is difficult to meet. They are not criminals, but they have no status. They don't trust banks, so when they begin to save money they carry it with them or they keep it in their rooms. They get robbed and burgled, but they are afraid to report the crimes because they are in the country illegally. Unscrupulous businessmen keep them in fear. They employ them, work them hard and then, on pay day, just before they are due to pay them their wages, they call the cops and report them as illegals. They get the work, and they don't pay the money. It leads to bitterness and more trouble.'

Inevitably, some of them do drift into crime. They steal cars and, although they have not driven before, they somehow cruise around, unlicensed and uninsured; and they become involved with gangs. Minor criminals are often deported, without having to serve a sentence, but return to the *barrio* in a day or two, having evaded the border patrol. Every day the deportation buses trundle across the border with their cargoes of illegals.

Some Americans grumble about the cross-border traffic and call for stricter measures. The border patrol is strengthened and a fence is put up and sensors are placed in the ground to detect footfalls. But there is a limit to what patrols can do; a fence means that a wetback has to walk an extra mile or two to get around it; and sometimes they steal the sensors.

Deportation is often self-defeating. Fathers and mothers are deported, while children get left behind; and deportation is often regarded by an established illegal alien as merely an interruption to a job. A girl working in a factory or an office may be found out by the immigration authorities and deported; but she tells her boss to keep her job open, and she comes back in a couple of days.

Once settled in, the illegal immigrant can get, with a little help from his friends, social security documents and perhaps a driving licence. If he is single and wants security he can get himself married to a girl whose status is good.

The United States, as I have remarked, is not committed wholeheartedly to stopping immigration. Deportation does not work, the police have no clear policy in respect of aliens and, although Anglo-Americans complain, the Mexican migrant, legal or illegal, is there to stay; and he is necessary.

In San Antonio one day I talked to leaders of the Mexican–American community. They were proud to have done the American thing: tugging at the bootstraps they had hauled themselves up, economically and socially. 'We are American,' they say, 'loyal, hard-working and home-loving. But we also want to keep a hold on our roots and culture. We want our religion to have an important place in our lives and to keep the Spanish language strong so that we can express ourselves not only in our everyday speech, but in our literature, poetry and songs. We have much to offer.'

A factory worker said: 'It is not always easy. There is still discrimination against Mexamericans and sometimes the police pick on us.

'It has been too easy for Mexican Americans to feel they are at the bottom and that they will always stay there. We have to fight against that sort of depression. Look, we say to our young people, you are human beings, the same as everyone else, and you have a great past. We tell them about their history, about the Aztec past, about the Spanish conquistadores, about the beauties of their Mexico, and how Mexico once extended into what is now the United States. We tell them about our role now, the work we do, and we show them the pictures of the Mexican Americans who are in the public eye: the scientists, the doctors, the politicians, the policemen, the film stars, the golfers — all the people who are Chicano and proud of it.

'We are a people beginning to move, to rediscover our pride. There are still people afraid of us, anxious about us because we are a little different, because we look a little different maybe. But we have our rightful place because we work hard. A lot of people have come to America and have had their turn — the Jews, the Irish, the Poles, a lot of people. And now, in the last twenty years of this century, it is our turn.'

17
THIS IS THE PLACE

There is only one religion, though there are a
hundred versions of it.

George Bernard Shaw

The train takes about fifteen hours to travel the five hundred
and seventy miles from Denver, state capital of Colorado, to
the oasis of Salt Lake City, state capital of Utah, which lies on
the other side of the Rocky Mountains. It is one of the great
remaining train rides. Three times a week the Rio Grande
Zephyr, drawn by two or three diesel-electric locomotives,
departs from Denver's Union Station in the chill before
breakfast-time and gathers its strength for the run at the mountains. It pants doggedly up the steeper inclines and seemingly
hauls itself hand over hand to make the tops of the slopes.
What a feat of railway building: at least a cut and a curse and a
bruise for every inch of the way. The train whistles through
numerous tunnels before plunging into the longest of them all,
the six-mile Moffat tunnel. It clings to the edges of great cliffs
and winds through red, brown and purple gorges. Around
here, in the last century, the gold and silver hunters who helped
to colonize this region by digging, panning and roistering,
found the wealth to found the state of Colorado. The track
runs through townships whose names evoke a frontier past:
Sulphur Springs, Troublesome, Radium and Rifle, and on into
Grand Junction. The Zephyr snakes along the valley of the
Colorado, past roaring falls and rapids where the swishing,
tumbling river, with streaming white mane, races the thudding
locomotives. After Grand Junction the Colorado takes its

158

leave and branches off south-west eventually to carve some more Grand Canyon; and the train heads into Utah, through Cisco, Solitude, Green River, Helper and Thistle; through Castle Gate where Butch Cassidy, in 1897, waited for the noon train and stole a company payroll of eight thousand dollars in gold and silver.

The work is easier as the train pushes through the haunting sage-brush desert, past cactus, scrub, isolated shacks and dried creeks, through sunset, swift twilight and starry darkness; until, at last, it wheezes, snorts, grumbles, sighs and gratefully subsides in the prim, pin-neat, fresh-swept capital of the Mormon faith and empire.

It is a three-meal journey and the food is agreeable enough. And there is a little bar where the bartender is friendly and enjoys chatting. The railroad is a thin wet line to a nearly dry city. Throughout the day the waiters, in white jackets and black trousers shiny as pewter, move through the dining car at slow and measured speed. They have made this journey for many years, so that the Rocky Mountains and all their vistas are etched in their souls. They have an obstinate dignity and move at their own pace. They cannot be hurried or bullied. As you wait for your order to come you watch the unfolding Rockies, and after a while the waiter emerges, moving with his tray at pallbearer pace. If the meal he sets in front of you were not the one you ordered, you would no doubt look into that patient face, and eat it up all the same. The dining car is comfortable and evokes a bygone age, before jets and interstate highways. You expect that at any minute young Bogart and Bacall will come in and sit down to dinner.

Actually it was a relief to hear the call of 'All aboard!' and chug out of Denver. I had been in the city a couple of days and I was anxious to get among the mountains, only twelve miles off and beckoning. Denver is a sprawling and bustling place, growing rapidly, and has about it an air of excitement, industry and purpose, as you would expect in a city, founded on mineral wealth in 1858, and now home for more than one and a half million people.

Denver is still a boom town. In the mountains lie nine-tenths of America's uranium reserves; and recent prospecting has revealed large reserves of oil, gas and coal. Big companies have been moving in and building their skyscrapers, and the businessmen's lunches at the Petroleum Club are full of earnest and bullish talk of drilling and surveying, of investment and backing hunches and dollars in their megamillions. As a sub-theme, a government mint in Denver rattles out millions of new coins a day.

Denver's boom makes it the fourth fastest growing city in the United States, and its location and prospects attract a great stream of immigrants. About a fifth of the people are Mexican Americans. Their leaders are working busily to improve the lot of these people, and are gradually wearing down discrimination. Children with a Mexican background make up nearly a third of the city's school population; and the Mexican flavour of Denver is found also in churches, music and restaurants. One of the attractions for visitors is an enormous Mexican restaurant which seats two thousand people. The food is served in a cafeteria production line fashion, so you move slowly down a line and accumulate tortillas, refried beans, enchiladas and guacamole, rather as a Ford on the line at Detroit accumulates doors, lights and wheels. The eating area is a great cavern done out like a jungle, with a waterfall, a pool and much shrubbery and greenery. High above the pool, on a little jutting stage, some men dressed as cowboys enact a western drama, with much shouting and cursing; and then they pull out revolvers and the cavern is filled with the roar of gunfire, and one of the cowboys falls backwards, plummeting to the pool, while you chew an enchilada. A small *mariachi* band arrives at the table, clad in sombreros, and corseted in tight black trousers with silver buttons down the seams. The players sing and thrum their guitars for a while before moving off to the next table. This is not the place where you would take a girl for a quiet candlelit evening intending to gaze into the liquid pools of her eyes.

Denver's location is enviable. The thirteenth step up to one of the doors of the state capitol is precisely a mile above sea level, hence Denver's nickname of Mile High City. The capitol's dome is plated with twenty-four carat Colorado gold, like a mosque's, and there are other pleasant buildings, like the city and county building, set amid swards and shrubs and trees. The skyscrapers, the museum, the art museum, the library where young employees speed around the stacks of books on roller skates, the huge performing arts centre are, like other institutions, part of the wealthy maturity and cultural swagger of a former frontier bonanza town which hasn't stopped bonanzing.

Denver exudes an air of bustle, purpose and open-air exuberance. On this high, dry, sunny plain there is an emphasis on sport and recreation, and the nearby Rockies provide some of the finest skiing anywhere. Up in the snows the brightly dressed ski-mad clamp on tape machines and earphones and, in response to the music only they can hear, swish and curve and jink and somersault downwards, lazily brilliant, their eyes seemingly closed as they fill themselves with the rhythms, the mountains and the pleasure of their own fit, thin and skilful bodies.

There is only one question mark over Denver's growth. Almost all its water comes from the melted snow in the Rockies, collected in reservoirs in the spring, and sometimes there has to be water rationing. Apart from that, Denver is a city blessed in many ways. And yet, a city so favoured is made ugly by air pollution which can smudge out the view of the mountains. Exhaust emissions, held down by the air currents, form a brown smog and make Denver's air the next most heavily polluted in the United States after Los Angeles. It is made ugly, too, by the agressive advertising that characterizes and damages so many American cities, and which in Denver, is particularly oppressive. The signs stand in groves and long lines as poplars do; but they are monstrous, floodlit, flashing. And the ones at the back are raised on substantial steel structures, like people at the back of a crowd jostling on tiptoe and waving.

The contrast, on entering Salt Lake City, is absolute. There are no bunches of crude and flashing signs here. In the wide avenues there is hardly a hoarding to be seen and what advertising there is is well-mannered and modest. It is part of the pleasing first impression of one of the most remarkable of American cities.

The place is manifestly clean and decent, a city that washes behind its ears and daily holystones its decks. In common with Denver it lies in a lovely and rugged setting, but it has more

respect for its surroundings and forbids commercial loutish-
ness to spoil it. It lies beneath the Wasatch Mountains which
are great ramparts, magnificent and strong and white-capped:
and there is about the city a crisp, crystal, alpine feel. In July
of 1847 Mormon refugees, fleeing religious persecution in
Illinois, arrived here after a heroic trek across the Great Plains
and through the Rocky Mountains. At the exit of Emigration
Canyon, their leader, Brigham Young, raised himself in the
wagon where he had been lying ill with fever. He saw the desert
valley of the Great Salt Lake.

'This,' he said, 'is the place.'

The phrase is honoured in Mormon history. In print it looks
bathetic, but at least it is more natural than those other famous
first words: 'That's one small step for man ... ' And Brigham Young, who no doubt felt that God had guided him and
his followers to the valley, presumably spoke the words with
enough emotion and drama for those within earshot to feel
them memorable.

Here, safe from hounding, on the bare canvas of the valley,
Brigham Young drew his city. The main street is a compass
needle, lying north and south, as it does in all Mormon towns,
and the other streets form a neat grid. The leader dictated that
they should be wide, and the pavements also. I fancied face-
tiously that, at twenty feet, the pavements were generous
enough in the polygamy years for a multi-wived Mormon to
walk his family abreast, like Tiller girls.

Four days after arrival in the valley, with his followers
already planting potatoes and building irrigation ditches,
Brigham Young, the Moses of his wandering tribe, jabbed at
the soil with his stick and ordered a temple built. It took forty
years to rise. The granite for it was hauled by oxen from quarries twenty miles off and the journey took four days for each
baulk. The temple has numerous spiky pinnacles and narrow
towers so that it resembles the kind of palace that used to illustrate fairy tales, or something that Disney drew. Outsiders, or
gentiles as the Mormons term them, may not enter it, but
photographs show us a place of opulence, with tall and
spacious chandeliered rooms and elegant furniture that seem
transplanted from Versailles; a grand duke or a Louis would
feel at home here. Its luxury is mirrored in other Mormon

temples whose soft carpeting, plush seating and fantastic murals are a far cry from bare-pewed architecture and furnishing.

Having drawn up his town plan and marked with the point of his stick the cornerstone of his temple, Brigham Young set about the creation of his astonishing co-operative society in the desert. Out of the dust was to grow a power in the land, a community which for its strength, its wealth, its totalitarianism, its evident clean living, its sexual nonconformity in straightlaced times, its sheer difference, has always been a focus for curiosity and prejudice and resentment.

The Mormons were like the Afrikaners. Fused solid by faith and difference, and by bullying, they trekked. By dint of dogged application of muscle and sinew, on a foundation of obstinacy, untroubled certainty and a certain arrogance, they succeeded in creating in an empty and hostile environment their singular civilization; succeeding where other 'ideal' American communities, like the one the Welsh socialist Robert Owen established in Indiana, ultimately failed.

The starting-point and central article of faith of the Mormon church seems flimsy to the gentile. But perhaps, paradoxically, that is also a strength: its tenuousness demands an element of defiant belief, and this, when shared, is a powerful adhesive. The church was only one of the fragments thrown out by a big bang of religious fervour in New York State in the 1820s and 1830s. A young man called Joseph Smith went around telling people that he had been visited by God and Christ who had told him that none of the existing religions were the true faith and that he would be heaven's agent for the restoration of the true church which had been lost hundreds of years before. Subsequently, he related, he was led by a heavenly messenger to some buried golden tablets on which were inscribed, in hieroglyphics, the words of the prophet Mormon. With the aid of magic spectacles young Mr Smith rendered the writings into English and published them as the Book of Mormon, a book which describes, in part, a migration of Jews to pre-Columbian America, and a visit by Christ to America. It is a strange story, Mr Smith's; lovingly told today in murals and dioramas and sound, and somewhat sticky commentary, at a church visitor centre in Salt Lake City. However curious, however difficult to believe, it is fundamental to the church.

In 1830, a small group of people, inspired by Joseph Smith, and hailing him as the prophet, joined with him to found the Church of Jesus Christ and the Latter-Day Saints. In the beginning the Mormons, as they were soon nicknamed, were an enigma; and, indeed, they are still. They were thrifty and hard-working and tended to prosper, and Joseph Smith said he had it on divine authority that polygamy was permitted. This upset people partly on religious grounds and partly, I imagine, because it was the cornering of the market in nubile lasses, a fairly scarce commodity in the pioneer west. Mormons put themselves outside the common run and were harassed by their intolerant fellow Americans. They eventually set up in Nauvoo, Illinois. Here a Welshman, John Griffiths, observed them in 1843 and wrote: 'We landed in a town called Nauvoo where Joe Smith and his Mormon followers are. It is only three years since this place was founded and there are about twenty-five thousand Mormons here already. Recently Joe was going to perform a miracle to fool the people by walking on the face of the waters. In the night he placed benches a foot below the surface but some trickster got to know about it and took one of the forms away. Next morning, crowds arrived to witness the miracle. Joe started walking very well, thinking that he would cross easily but suddenly he went head first to the bottom. I heard that Joe was in prison.'

Smith, indeed, was later dragged from jail and murdered and martyred. Big, bearded Brigham Young took charge. He was altogether a stronger character, one of nature's khans, bold and brave, a shrewd organizer who knew how to inspire and to rule by ukase. He led one hundred and forty-eight men, women and children for fourteen hundred miles across the plains from Illinois before ruling that Salt Lake valley, then part of Mexico, was The Place. The State of Deseret, the Mormons called it, the honey-bee state; and many were relieved that they were far from their foes, that they had quit the United States, land of the free.

Some of those who followed on were delighted with the new life they found. 'I have been blessed beyond what I could expect,' wrote Sam Evans in 1854. But a fellow Welshman, Evan Howell, had long tired of Mormons and wrote to a friend: 'I beg you to use all your influence with my friends and the people of Wales to prevent them becoming blinded by such a system of roguery and plunder as Mormonism.'

The Mormons tamed the desert by making it a huge collective farm and by irrigating it with water that was under community management. They tamed it by being ruthlessly hard-working, by praying hard and sticking together under autocratic Brigham Young. Such a hostile land could not have been settled at that time by the haphazard rugged individualism that characterized much western settlement. With an endurance that matched their faith, Mormons were the prime force behind the establishment of scores of towns in the southwestern United States; and, with the railroads, they were the main agencies of settlement in the region in the second half of the nineteenth century.

As they ploughed and greened their oasis Zion, the Mormons, the Moonies of their day, were more than objects of interest. Their success made them objects of envy, but their practice of polygamy made them objects of wonder, and also revulsion. Brigham Young himself set a notable example: he had twenty-seven wives and fathered fifty-six children by sixteen of them.

To some followers, however, particularly the women, polygamy was demeaning and caused unhappiness. 'As to polygamy,' a woman wrote from Utah to a friend in Wales in 1862, '*you* are without a dread of anyone claiming a share with you; this dread has made me so miserable in past times that I almost wished myself at the bottom of the sea, instead of in Utah, but so far I have been spared that trial! You cannot conceive what women have to suffer here with a view to obtain some greater glory hereafter, which I for one am willing to forgo ... '

One might imagine what popular newspapers today would make of it all if authorized polygamy still existed. As it was this most publicized of the Mormons' differentia excited a wide variety of reactions among those fascinated and frightened by sex: grundyism, prurience and censoriousness being pre-eminent. The question of polygamy was used as a stick to beat the Mormons and it eventually became the key issue in the matter of Utah statehood. It became clear that the Mormons could not remain a polygamous island, nor could they stay fenced off from wider America in economic and social terms.

In the event the United States enacted laws to prohibit plural marriage; and multi-spoused Mormon leaders were arrested. There was a bitter struggle lasting nearly thirty years. The government was fought all the way to the Supreme Court; but, in 1890, the court found against the Mormons and the 'everlasting covenant' of polygamy, ordained in Mormon scripture, was ended. The Mormon leadership found that it could renounce what had been an important tenet and henceforth polygamists were to be excommunicated. It was part of the entry fee to the burgeoning America and, with this pillar of the faith fallen, the church ceased to be a collective, sloughed off the skin of church socialism, began to trade widely with gentiles and allowed the co-operatives to pass into private ownership. Mormons went wholeheartedly into profit-making and adopted the thrusting laissez-faire attitudes and practices of their compatriots. In short, they became fully paid-up Americans.

In 1896 Utah joined the club and got its statehood. Its sobriquet is the Beehive State and its motto is Industry; a fitting label for the worker bees.

In the Beehive House, Brigham Young's handsome mansion in Salt Lake City, where the old master ruled, I had lunch with some members of the church. They said that some small breakaway groups still practise the old proscribed custom and take a number of wives, and added, with small wry smiles, that the Mormon connection with polygamy still fascinated gentiles.

We discussed business as well, but the Mormons quietly and smilingly and politely drew a curtain. The church is immensely rich, and if most of us do not care how rich, Mormons and their corporate wealth are a constant source of interest for journalists. The Associated Press has estimated that the Church of Latter-Day Saints has an income of three million dollars a day; but Mormons say nothing and pass you the water and ask if you have had enough apple pie. In any case, the exact extent of the church's riches is a secret known to only fifteen of the hierarchy. No financial statement is published and tithes are not itemized. As for the average Utahan — and seven-tenths of Utahans are Mormons — I suspect that most of them are like those I talked to: they simply do not regard the subject as important.

The church is now among the leading wealthy corporations of the United States because its members pay a tenth of their gross income to the organization, because the money is invested wisely in land and businesses and because the ministry is unpaid. The church owns, or has substantial interest in, thirteen radio and television stations, a newspaper, stores, insurance companies, farms, ranches, hotels and development companies. The church office building in Salt Lake City is a glass and steel pillar of the faith, twenty-eight storeys high and the tallest building in the city. From the top is a marvellous view of Brigham Young's kingdom, the snowy Wasatch peaks and the flat valley floor stretching off to the lake in the distance. Several floors of the tower are devoted to the acquisition and management of property.

Under the canopy of business and corporate affluence, the church remains strongly family-oriented, community-minded, patriarchal and obedient, just as it was when the Latter-Day Saints went marching in and yoked themselves together to plough and drill. And it still retains a link with its co-operative past, a welfare safety net for its adherents. The church has no time for state welfare. 'Faithful Latter-Day Saints shun government welfare and rely on church welfare only when absolutely necessary,' it says. The Mormon's own welfare system was started in the 1930s with the aim of doing away with 'the curse of idleness and the evils of dole ... work is to be re-enthroned as the ruling principle of the lives of our church membership ... '

Congregations are encouraged to find jobs for those who need them and to look after those of their fellows who fall on hard times. The bishops, who are lay leaders of congregations, can call on members to forgo a meal or two and donate the cost to welfare funds. 'In one year,' I was told by a church official, 'we have given twenty-three million dollars worth of assistance to one hundred and thirty thousand of our members who needed help. A person entitled to help gets a bishop's order and goes to a bishop's storehouse, a sort of supermarket, and gets what he needs. He hands over no money. There are no cash registers.' Food is grown on church farms, and volunteers help to sow and hoe. Cans and other goods in the bishops' storehouses are marked with the Deseret label and are ferried about the country by the lorries and vans of Deseret Transportation.

It is part of the warm enveloping blanket of the church. Mormonism is a complete way of life. It protects its followers from many of the confusions and difficulties and decisions of our era by providing a strong framework for living and an emphasis on family and congregational activity. It demands a literal belief in the story of Joseph Smith and the golden tablets, or at least a tight rein on doubts, a belief that the elders of the church know best, and simple obedience. The twelfth of the thirteen Mormon articles of faith states: 'We believe in being subject to kings, presidents, rulers and magistrates, in obeying, honouring and sustaining the law.'

The stable, ordered way of life is evidently attractive. The church has grown fourfold in thirty years and now numbers about four million members throughout the world. In an America where many young people have been assailed by doubt and confusion, and have sought solace and purpose in numerous versions of Christianity, the Mormon church has been the fastest-growing faith. Not only does it provide the rules and strong leadership that many people seem to want, it appears to be a chinkless carapace in an uncertain world. The church is pervasive in home and social life, so that Mormons spend their time working, conversing, playing and praying with other Mormons. It lays down rules of personal behaviour, prohibiting alcohol, smoking and the drinking of tea and coffee, and encourages exercise. Mormons are significantly less susceptible than other Americans to cancer, heart disease and diabetes. The state of Utah has the lowest cancer rate of all the United States and the death rate from heart attacks among Mormons is between one third and one half of the national average. Avoidance of alcohol and tobacco are important factors and so, presumably, are Mormon dietary rules which insist on considerable fruit consumption, place an emphasis on grain and call for a one-day fast every month.

'I believe that the quality of the food has a lot to do with the long life of the people of Utah. The food here is so good that most of the inhabitants eat only two meals a day, breakfast and supper, but remember that they are not the scanty meals of the Old Country but plenty of variety of delicacy,' a Mormon settler wrote home in the 1870s. Presumably, too, a well-ordered way of life without much stress plays its part in Mormon health.

The church keeps its young members busy with an intensive social, sporting and cultural programme and thousands of them are trained to be missionaries and to work overseas for two years trying to recruit more members. In common with many people in Britain I have encountered those fresh-faced and earnest young men who knock at your door just as you are beginning dinner, and who try to interest you in the golden tablets. I have always found them, not simply other-worldly, almost too perfectly clean-cut and pinkly scrubbed, but also impenetrable. They reveal nothing of themselves, as if their human warmth was sealed off, and they seem incapable of normal conversation, ploughing ahead like programmed encyclopaedia salesmen. They always put me in mind of the rocket ship personnel in the old BBC radio serial *Journey Into Space* who, their minds held captive, could only answer questions by saying: 'Orders are orders and must be obeyed without question at all times.'

One Sunday morning, in Salt Lake City, I saw a group of them being farewelled as they set off on proselytizing tours around the world. Their hair as short as Marines' combat cuts, sober-suited and weeping, they stood beneath the dome of the tabernacle. This is a remarkable circular building which seats more than six thousand people and where the renowned Mormon Tabernacle choir performs under a nail-less roof secured by rawhide.

So perfect are the acoustics that, from anywhere in the tabernacle, you may hear a pin drop on the stage. Indeed, a guide will prove it. He asks you to stand some distance from the stage, extracts a pin from a yellow pincushion kept for the purpose in the wings, and drops it; and, sure enough, you can hear it. On this Sunday morning, in this place of flawless sound, the three hundred and seventy-five members of the Tabernacle choir were seated on the stage singing silkily beneath the gigantic organ: it was another of the smoothly packaged Sunday radio programmes which have been broadcast from this place for half a century. The young missionaries and their families had tears rolling down their faces. Called to service by their church, they were off to the earth's corners to spread Joseph Smith's message. They, their parents and their friends, were paying all the bills for this missionary work, not the church.

The Mormon church was a racialist church. Its scriptures taught that a black skin was the mark of Cain, a curse visited on the descendants of Cain for his slaughter of Abel. In the Mormon visitor centre in Salt Lake City I saw that someone had written in the visitors' book: 'What about the blacks?' I took this up with one of my Mormon hosts at lunch and he shifted uneasily and passed the water and said, with a shake of the head: 'You will never understand. How can you possibly understand?' I persisted and he said that black people could join the church but they could not achieve full membership and join the lay priesthood. This meant they were disqualified from getting to heaven's hierarchy.

The discrimination caused years of tensions within the church. Many young Mormons, in particular, felt conscience-stricken. They thought that their church was out of step with the times. At last, in 1978, with pressure growing from within and without for the removal of the offensive bar on black people, the church's president announced a divine revelation: black men could now be full members and get into the heavenly hierarchy. At such a timely revelation many Mormons breathed a sigh of relief.

No ordinary member of the church would seriously question the president's ruling. The church is run by a theocracy and the president is considered to be God's prophet, with a line to the Almighty. He heads the church's main authority, the Quorum of the Twelve Apostles, who see to it that the organization grows larger and stronger. They tend to be big businessmen and are perfectly content that the church's writ runs in political and economic matters in the state of Utah. Church and state cannot be separated and church influence is omnipresent. Few gentiles have represented Utah in Congress. The church leaders confidently take strongly conservative positions on most issues, and have steadily steered their followers further to the right. They have emphatically anti-liberal views on law and order, welfare, unions, women's rights and minority rights.

The influential leaders of the church are not only the heads of a theocracy; they are also the hidebound grey heads in a gerontocracy. Brigham Young, who went to the heavenly hierarchy in 1877, himself stipulated that presidents should reach the job by virtue of seniority and the law of Buggins' Turn has never been questioned. When the church president died in 1970, aged ninety-six, his successor was ninety-three. The leader who had the revelation admitting black men was eighty-four, with a man nearly eighty waiting in the wings; a man, incidentally, who is a member of the extreme right-wing group, the John Birch Society, which is against almost everything, and certainly would not have allowed any revelation concerning blacks to enter *his* made-up and laced-up mind.

Nor would he, nor would most Mormons, contemplate a radical change in the place of women in their framework of living. Women are subordinate and their role is defined clearly. As mothers and home-makers their job is to be at home. The church holds that the man is the superior being because he may enter the lay priesthood — a woman may not — and through this priesthood derives the spiritual power which makes him wiser. The church is opposed to the idea of equal rights for women, seeing this as a recipe for instability. Nevertheless, the question of the subordination of women will tick away, just as the question of blacks did; and while change seems inconceivable at the moment, there must be the possibility of an accommodating revelation in the future.

While Mormons have taken steps to integrate, there are those in the church, a small minority, concerned about Mormon apartness. I had dinner one night with a Mormon academic who was profoundly anxious about his church's reactionary outlook. 'It is for me a time of anguish. My wife has recently renounced the church after a lifetime of membership — '

'I feel liberated,' she broke in. 'After years I feel that at last I belong to myself. Breaking with the church was the hardest thing I have ever done, but now I have a freedom of spirit I have never known before. It is not easy to get away. I'm not popular because of what I have done and my children, who are believers, are very upset. And the habits are so hard to break. Do you know, I had to make an effort to get coffee for you tonight. Coffee, as you know, is not permitted by the church and I feel very strange offering it to you. I've never done it before. But I won't have any myself. Some of the influences are hard to get away from, and I would still feel guilty if I drank coffee!'

Her husband said: 'I've been a loyal member, but I think I have been suspect for some time because of my questioning attitude. I have to say that I am wrestling with my conscience because I can no longer believe the story of Joseph Smith. I know all the stories about him, that he introduced polygamy because he was going with another woman and wanted to institutionalize adultery. For a long time that did not matter. But I have lost belief in the story of the tablets and Joseph Smith. Yet there is much that is good in this church. It is a wonderful power for good and for happiness. But there is a danger that it will split because the leadership is old and out of step with modern thinking.'

Most Mormons, though, are not troubled by such doubts. They find enough fulfilment in carrying out their responsibilities to church, family and their ancestors. Mormons take part in a bizarre form of ancestor-worship as an extension of their love of family. To them the family includes the twigs and branches on the family tree, even if it stretches back for centuries. A good Mormon will collect the evidence of his ancestors' existence and will be the proxy by which these dead kith are baptized; so that, in heaven, families will be enormous and united for eternity.

To this end the Mormon church has assembled the largest genealogical library in the world, containing millions of records of births, marriages and deaths. In thirty-five countries there are microfilm photographers steadily working their way through registers and sending their harvest to Salt Lake City for filing. The storehouses for the records, for the four thousand rolls of microfilm that arrive every month, are vast. In Salt Lake City there is a genealogical library and, twenty miles away, most remarkable of all, there is a mighty underground silo built to last until doomsday. It is hollowed deep in the granite of a mountain and the microfilm files lie in green steel cabinets in vaults sealed with bank doors weighing nine tons. The place is nuclear-proof and has cost millions of dollars. There are computers and closed-circuit television and

172

security guards; and there is water and food to supply the staff of eighty, should disaster strike. And all the time Mormons are working loyally and tenaciously to find their grandfathers's grandfather's grandfather, to have him baptized, to give him a place in heaven.

When you think about it, it is quite astonishing.

But then, Salt Lake City is remarkable. Its broad avenues and trees, its prospering and well-ordered commerce, its lack of commercial vulgarity, give it an aura of wholesomeness that I found in few other places in the United States: Disney World in Florida was one other. I never found a bar in Salt Lake City, though I bought a beer at a petrol station. I found a pool hall, but its sinfulness was mitigated by its bar which stocked no alcohol, only soft drinks. I heard that a cinema had tried to show a film that the Mormons considered pornographic, and they had picketed the cinema and forced the withdrawal of the film. Sin, though, has its way of peeking through, and, one morning, I went to buy newspapers and entered a large newsagent and bookstore. Most of the shop was empty, but there was a small cordoned corral marked Adults Only where there were displayed *Playboy* and the like. The men in there were packed shoulder to shoulder, like beef cattle in a stockyard.

In the end, Salt Lake City is a phenomenon. All this city, this empire, from an unlikely young man's unlikely story, a story that dares you to believe it. Among the Mormons I met there I found an always smiling welcome and a great willingness to discuss most aspects of the church and its works. But the shutters went down at once when I began to dig nearer the foundations of their beliefs, as if the questions themselves would corrode the faith. 'You do not understand,' they would smile, a shade insecurely, and move to safer ground. As for the religious buildings in the city itself, I had thought I might find there the atmosphere of holiness that pervades many sacred places in the world — cathedrals, shrines and places of worship — whatever the faith. But here I found none of that. Of course, as a gentile I was not admitted to the temple; but I was struck in Brigham Young's city by the atmosphere of employee-loyalty and unquestioning devotion, of protected values and conservative outlook, that one might find in a large, old-fashioned, slightly eccentric, family firm.

18
APPLE PIPS

Purple-robed and pauper-clad,
Raving, rotting, money-mad;
A squirming herd in Mammon's mesh,
A wilderness of human flesh;
Crazed with avarice, lust and rum,
New York, thy name's Delirium.

Byron Rufus Newton

If you are fortunate you arrive over New York at dusk, and marvel, as the wing dips, at the shimmering electric beauty of Manhattan in its suit of lights. The pilot says: 'Great view of Manhattan tonight, folks.' There is a hint of proprietorial pride in his voice, as if he had arranged it all himself, like a good host. The sight of coruscating crystal palaces emerging on tiptoe from the indigo is a true pleasure, one to flatten your nose for; and one that should be savoured as an interlude of blessed calm and sweet fantasy before you land at Kennedy airport. For here the bright jolly-nurse stewardesses smile good-bye and the planes unload their people, as if upending sacks of beans into a silo.

The alien beans are filtered through sorting racks called immigration gates. The immigration officer looks through a vast directory to check that you are not wanted for murder, tax fiddling or insulting the Stars and Stripes and motions you through. 'Have a terrific trip.' Outside there is confusion, as if people are being sucked helter-skelter helpless into a whirlpool. The air is thick with exhaust fumes and people are pink with carbon monoxide, fear, fatigue and embarrassment. There is withal a heavy dust of bustle; and a loud noise made of shouts, oaths and anxious questions, as teeming hundreds bounce and change direction like bagatelle balls. Taxis are whistled up by patrolmen and they come nosing in alongside the fretting queues. The taxis, yellow, scratched and dented, are piloted by drivers who look world-weary and irritated and late for their supper. They lurch and barge their way into vacant spaces. The drivers stick out their heads and shout. Policmen shout. Couriers shout. Porters and passengers shout. Everybody shouts.

'Move on for crissakes.'
'Get out for crissakes.'
'That dumb broad.'
'You joking mister?'
'Get that jerk outa here.'
'Move over you son of a bitch.'
'Because it's my rights that's why.'
'Jesus, you deaf buddy?'
'Listen lady, this ain't no charity.'
'No need to make a federal case out of it.'
'Don't give me that bullshit, buddy.'
'For crissakes.'

You soon learn that shouting and altercation are part of the social currency of New York, a tradition. Many people seem to enjoy an abrasive encounter. You also learn swiftly that New Yorkers are always right. The best way to undermine them is to apologize abjectly: they are not used to this and they feel uncomfortable. At the airport, though, there is not much time for apology. Buses and hotel vans and limousines pile in like forwards into a ruck. The taxi-drivers snarl and knit their brows. The bus drivers bellow, the van drivers spit and roar. Little shoals of startled Japanese, with neat mackintoshes and lemonade-bottle spectacles, dart like minnows. Stetsoned Texans shoulder through. Blue-rinsed matrons screech like parakeets. Nuns look reproachful, as if the Almighty is testing their patience too far. Small groups of businessmen, with their abbreviated nether integuments, coagulate; pale, disapproving, tired, muttering 'For crissakes' to each other.

The second time I arrived in New York I was with my wife and we took the four-dollar bus ride from the airport into Manhattan. From the bus station we had to take a taxi across town to the hotel. Outside the terminus there was a chirpy cab driver who helped us load our baggage into the boot of the familiar yellow cab. A fat man with glasses approached and said: 'Say, I'm going the same way as you folks. Can I ride along?'

I said he could and he got into the front seat, turning round to talk to us as the taxi bucked along over the potholes.

'You folks from England? I just love that country. Just love the people. Real law-abiding people. Is that right your cops don't carry guns? Isn't that something. Makes me feel real ashamed of New York. There are people here who would kill you for ten cents. It's a crazy city. People would kill their mother and they get away with it. The cops can't catch anybody. The place is full of crazies. Drug addicts, killers, pimps. You name it, New York has it. It ain't no place for decent people any more. You can't bring up kids here. The crazies burn the schools and beat up the teachers and the kids are onto drugs in grade school. If they don't end up on drugs, they end up in prison or they get mugged. Everybody gets mugged. Grandmothers get mugged. You own grandmother ain't safe in this city, you know that. You know, I feel really bad about my country when I see nice people like you coming here. I feel ashamed, I really do.'

He chatted on in this fashion, a fat and friendly Mr Nice as Mr Chirpy the taxi driver steered carefully into the potholes so that the cab lurched constantly.

'Isn't that right, this is a terrible place for crime,' Mr Nice said.

'Crazy,' Mr Chirpy agreed.

'Crazy?' said Mr Nice. 'Crazy ain't it. The crime makes me sick to my stomach, it really does.'

At last we drew up at the hotel. 'Hope you folks have a really swell time,' Mr Nice said. 'I'll help you with your bags.'

I asked Mr Chirpy what the fare was. 'Forty-three dollars,' he said. I had estimated the fare at three or four dollars.

'You must be joking.'

Mr Chirpy looked hurt. 'I am not joking, sir. That is the official New York fare.'

'Well I'm not paying it.'

Mr Chirpy's face darkened and he was transformed in an instant to Mr Weasel. And the amiable expression had been switched off in Mr Nice's face. He was now a threatening Mr Nasty, Mr Weasel's Myrmidon. And I knew that sinking, face-flushing feeling a man knows when he has been a mug. The cab had no meter and was on routine rip-off patrol when it happened on two likely marks from England. Mr Nasty was reaching inside his coat and I knew I would see the gun that all the films, newspaper stories and melodramas I had seen about New York now led my imagination to expect. Mr Nasty, however, produced a printed card which read: Official Taxi Fares. 'Forty-three dollars,' he said. Both he and Mr Weasel seemed prepared to be a shade difficult about the matter. It was a question of getting out of the car, getting my wife safely out, getting our hostage luggage out of the boot. They backed off a little when I said I knew they were operating illegally without a meter. But in the end we bargained and it cost sixteen dollars to get the luggage out; an uneasy transaction.

Mr Nasty pocketed the money.

Mr Weasel glared and turned the ignition key.

'Limeys,' said Mr Nasty.

'Welcome to New York,' the hotel desk clerk said.

2

New York is a city of strong flavours, of gasps and not sighs. It feeds you on mustard and tabasco sauce and makes you main-line on adrenalin. It is not possible to be neutral about it. It has a thumping heart. It is dramatic, startling, exciting, fast, lurid, huge and magnificent. Almost everything you have heard about it is largely true. There is not much of the qualities of gentleness and langour in New York. It is, in essence, stride city, not stroll city. Its pulse rate and blood pressure stay high. It is not a city of curves, whorls and ellipses: there is nothing softly Celtic about its shapes, aspects and demeanour. Rather, it is jutting, thrusting, sharp and abrassive. Its vagrant winds rolling down its canyons whip and slap, not caress. It puts grit in your eye and it spits in your eye. It is challenging, raw and edgy. So I found it exhilarating.

In common with most foreigners, when I talk of New York I mean Manhattan, the island Peter Minuit bought from Indians for twenty-four dollars worth of beads in 1626; and not the boroughs of Brooklyn, the Bronx, Queens and Staten Island, the boroughs where most New Yorkers live.

It is in Manhattan that the people, by building, demolishing, rebuilding and pushing and shoving, have created a city of constantly changing aspect that reflects the upsurge of all America; restless and upward reaching. Manhattan is a bed of steel and concrete reeds. The banks and business houses stand in great soaring ranks: Mammon's sentries. They made me feel like an ant looking up at a taut regiment of Guards. They make New York a symbol of triumphant and powerful capitalism. And you may ascend to the tops of even higher skyscrapers and look down on these giants. There is nothing else for it but to marvel. And although the geminate towers of the World Trade Center are taller, the view from the Empire State Building is better, to my mind, because it is closer to the centre and the drama, because it seems taller.

Ella Fitzgerald sings that 'the great big city's a wondrous toy, just made for a girl and boy.' And so it is. The pleasures of New York are beyond number. They exhaust the brain, sate the mind and wear out shoe leather. There is about this city a ceaseless throbbing, as in a power station. New Yorkers like to think they are *blasé* about it, but their pride in it and the recognition of the romance in it keeps showing through. One afternoon the driver of the taxi I was in turned around and with a spontaneous expansive gesture said: 'Isn't New York just fantastic?' And that evening, in a flat high above Central Park, my host stretched his arm to indicate the lofty sequinned towers twinkling all around and said: 'Isn't New York just something?'

Yes it is. Though I've seen only fragments of it. New York is not only very American, it is also strikingly non-American: for it is, more than most, a city of foreigners, with a rich jumble of origins. Its people have built themselves oases and enclaves for their colours, tongues, religions, inclinations, income, diet and preferences. The range of restaurants is vast: you may taste your way around the planet in Manhattan's twenty-two square miles; you may sniff the cookpots of the world. Just by riding in taxis you may see something of New York's ethnic scatter: there are twelve thousand taxis and in each one the driver's photograph and name can be seen through the anti-robbery screen. They are the names of the world.

Although it appears that way at first sight, New York is not

178

entirely frenetic. It is a city of music, drama, art, museums, sights, relaxations and quite gentle entertainments. It should be said that it has its pools of charm, its boltholes, its recesses, its off-duty places like refuges behind a front-line trench. It is pleasant to buy a sandwich for lunch and sit and listen to accents; and sandwiches in New York are not only large and satisfying, but of infinite variety; and it is easy to get flustered by the variety of fillings and breads on offer when ravenous New Yorkers are behind you in the queue. It is pleasant to watch skaters on the ice at Rockefeller Center, to take the boat excursion around Manhattan island, to pay twenty-five cents for a ride on the Staten Island ferry, to walk in Central Park on a warm afternoon or a crisp morning, to eat omelettes and drink leafy Bloody Marys for Sunday brunch, that most civilized of meals and institutions, to take coffee and the *New York Times* in small cafes, to be given a ticket for a Broadway show that you otherwise could not afford, to take thin beer with jazz, to find a happy busy restaurant that does not leave your wallet hurt, to buy a pretzel from the street barrow, to talk over whiskey sours in shadowy bars, to see haughty Manhattan girls, black and white, walking by. Hearing that Radio City music hall was about to close down, I hurried to it to see for myself a piece of authentic Americana before it was lost for ever. It was a vast plush cavern, like the great Gaumonts of my boyhood, only bigger; and there were the Rockettes, thirty-six closely linked dancing girls forged into a machine evoking an age of stricter mores, anachronistic in their wholesomeness. I heard later that they were still going strong — if other historical pieces can be preserved, why not the Rockettes? — so perhaps, as in some shops, their closing-down sale will last for ever.

I have visited New York both at the enervating peak of summer and the marrow-freezing depths of winter. New Yorkers have found they can cheat the seasons with air-conditioning and central heating; but, as is the American way, they tend to excess. In winter in New York it would be possible to work in shorts, so hot is the central heating. In summer, so cold is the air from the iron lungs of the air conditioning that a thick jacket is needed to prevent shivering. With restrictions on the supply of oil, New Yorkers may have to wear vests and woolly socks in winter, and slow down a shade in summer.

The soft life, though, has led directly to one of the great sounds of New York, the slapslap-puffpuff sound of the morning joggers as they trot by. They do it for their health, of course, to counterbalance the effect of easy living; though I suspect, judging by their tortured faces, they do it as a kind of atonement, a self-flagellation, for their comfort. Some jog out of shame. Because Americans do not do things by halves they have thrown themselves into jogging with earnest determination and, as an indication of how seriously they regard it, they have renamed it running. There is now a jogging industry selling magazines, books, shoes, watches and pedometers. And, scenting a good thing, the psychiatrists have moved in. Some go out jogging with their patients, saying this is a novel way of penetrating the subconscious. One jogging head-shrinker is said by a jogging magazine to be 'a therapeutic messiah who will lead the mentally disturbed out of the desert.' On the evidence of some of the books on sale, it is plain that jogging is becoming metaphysical as well as physical. Perhaps that is why so many joggers look so glazed as they bash round Central Park. In the same way that it is wrong to try to waken a somnambulist, it is perhaps dangerous to try to talk with a New York jogger. For most of them jogging has become an obsession. They ignore their running injuries, their bruised feet, ankles and knees. They blink back the tears caused by joggers' nipple, the result of jogging vests abrading these tender spots. I read of a man in New England who insisted on running in his scanties in very cold weather and, complaining of pain, was advised by his doctor that he had a touch of penile frostbite; so that's enough about jogging.

Except to add by way of postscript that jogging is part of the colour of New York. It helps to give the city a more human aspect, like the little carnivals, the street musicians, the street corner jugglers, the concrete chess tables built by the parks department, the games of bowls played in odd corners, the pagoda-shaped telephone booths in Chinatown, the ladies obeying the new ordinance and following their pesky dogs with shovels and patent scoops: though why anyone should want to keep a mutt in Manhattan is beyond me.

New York is called the Big Apple because it is rich in

opportunity, dollars, culture, business and fun. But the apple is also maggoty. Anything that can go wrong in modern civilization has gone wrong in New York. It is, in parts, an eaten-out hulk, poor, rotting and a dead end. The contrasts are astonishing. Wealth sits thigh by thigh with wretchedness, the beautiful within hand's reach of the hideous. New Yorkers feel pride in their city, but also shame. As you walk on the sunny side of the street you may pick up a newspaper and read of more violence, of the high murder rate, of homeless children who are apprentice thieves and prostitutes, of arsonists and bandits.

In the narcotics department of the New York City Police they told me that inflation had pushed up the price of a street dose of heroin from forty-four to fifty-one dollars; though hardly anyone calls it heroin — in the drugs market it is called scag, smack, thing, doojee, harry, caballo, boy, chinese red, mexican mud, big H. 'So much money is involved in drugs that no one believes the trade can be stopped,' a detective said. 'The crime and ill-health that are caused by the illicit drugs industry cost this country billions upon billions of dollars. Kids here grow up in heroin-oriented societies. An addict needs at least fifty dollars a day to support his habit, and either he's on welfare or he's getting his money through crime. It's said that sixty per cent of crime here is drug-related. People get so rich at the drugs game that they can easily put up a hundred thousand dollars' bail, and more, and flee the country. It's an endless and unwinnable war. One of the best things society can do is educate the kids, show what a mess drugs make of lives, and treat the addicts and help us to enforce the law. There's no easy answer.' They told me in narcotics about a drug baron aged fifteen who enjoyed wealth and power. Too young to have a driving licence, he had to have his own driver.

No part of New York is more ravaged than south Bronx. 'Why you going out to south Bronx? You crazy?' the taxi driver asked. 'The place is all shot up, all burned out. You know what? When the cops go on patrol they take lions and gorillas for company. The lions do the arresting and the gorillas do the searching.'

The district reminded me of the bombed parts of British cities I knew. The people have been burning their tenement blocks so that they can be moved into better municipal housing, and the landlords have been burning property to collect insurance and evade taxes. In this dreadful place people struggle for existence. Some of them are beggars. Their lives are fouled by high unemployment, poverty, drug addiction and trafficking, by racial violence, squalor and gang rule. As I walked through the streets I sensed a pervading air of depression, hopelessness and resentment; and in the people's unsmiling faces was sullenness and suspicion. I returned to Manhattan by way of the drab and dirty subway and tried to decipher the graffiti which covers almost every inch of every carriage, inside and out. Graffiti artists in New York, and in other cities, like Philadelphia and Chicago, have almost joined the mass communications industry.

Throughout the city cars were jolting over large potholes in ill-kept streets and the talk in the papers and elsewhere was of New York's chronic financial trouble. It was the inevitable result of mismanagement of the city's finances, a large and badly administered welfare programme, the flight of business, brains and capital from the city. There was large-scale unemployment and difficulties and costs that arose from New York's traditional role as magnet and conduit for immigrants. Its former middle-class and lower-middle-class areas had fallen into disrepair as people had moved out to the suburbs. The city had to seek help from the government, and more than a few Americans enjoyed New York's discomfiture. For New York has always irritated the people of wider America: New Yorkers have always seemed to them to adopt a certain superior air. 'What's so great about New York?' is what many Americans say. 'I wouldn't live there if you paid me — it's dirty, dangerous, riddled with crime, decadent, full of slums. And the city government has bungled.' A lot of people agree with Byron Rufus Newton that New York is :

> Vulgar of manner, overfed,
> Overdressed and underbred;
> Heartless, Godless, hell's delight.

and throughout America the emotional response to New York's cries for help was a sniffy 'Let it squirm.'

Squirm it did. But New York is muscular and began to pull

out of its fiscal quagmire. The morale of New Yorkers began to brighten. They felt that, for all its scars and rotten places, New York had a magic that was working again, that the shine could be put back on their apple.

19
SHRINES BUILT AND HEROES BORN

God reigns, and the Government at Washington lives!

James Abram Garfield

After a while I had had enough of adrenalin and mustard and decided to catch a train to Washington for a change of air and diet. I went to bright and efficient Pennsylvania station, 'at a quarter to four,' as the song suggested, and bought a ticket and a magazine. A soft voice announced: 'The Metroliner to Washington is leaving from West Gate Ten,' — and added in a low sing-song: 'A-a-a-ll aboard!'

There is a certain romance about American railways, which is no doubt felt more by foreigners. The railways were for so long the country's veins and the story of the trains is a large part of the story of America. And, still, even in the jet age, there is a greater sense of adventure and exploration in boarding a long-distance train than in catching a plane. There is a sense of scale and distance about a railway, a sense distorted by air travel. And the long-haul trains still carry proper romantic names, like the South Crescent which runs from New York to Atlanta, Silver Meteor from New York to Miami, the Palmetto from New York to Savannah. And there is the Night Owl, the Montrealer, the Bankers, the Flying Yankee, Hilltopper, Senator and Patriot.

Romance, unfortunately, is never enough. Passenger railways in the United States had their peak in 1916 when they carried ninety-eight per cent of all inter-city travellers. But after the Second World War competition from road and air transport pushed the railways increasingly into crisis. In 1971 the government set up Amtrak, a public corporation, to keep essential passenger services going, but it inherited a network from private companies which badly needed modernizing. The companies were compensated for handing over the money-losing routes and they retained control of their freight lines which are profitable; so that Amtrak was built on sand. Amtrak has been doing its best to improve its services, but its cause is not a popular one and it does not have enough champions in government. To save money the government is being urged to do more of what Dr Beeching did to railways in Britain: amputate on a large scale. Today only one per cent of Americans take a train for their inter-city journeys; and Amtrak's losses continue to mount. Nevertheless the railways may still have useful future, and on a large scale. There is a growing number of voices talking about the advantages of rail transport, its safety, its comfort, its lack of pollution. And as petrol becomes more expensive the pro-railway argument strengthens.

The Metroliner took three hours to cover the two hundred and twenty-four miles from the heart of New York to the heart of Washington. The guard announced: 'In three minutes we shall be arriving in Union Station, Washington DC, the home of Jimmy Carter. Thank you for travelling Amtrak. Have a nice evening.' The train slid into the cool, vast and airy temple of Union Station, most majestic of gateways, now refurbished as the National Visitor Center. It was built in 1907 to shelter great crowds and its style is American-Roman Grand: tall columns, a high arched roof, vaulting, clean lines and much statuary: very Washington. Among its many services is a dazzling multi-projector presentation of American history and beauty, with suitably stirring musical accompaniment; and, indeed, the entire splendid building is determined to uplift and impress. In this it succeeds; and in this too, it is part of the essence of Washington. It is as if the city has been getting back at those early critics who sniggered and wrote so cuttingly of it.

And snigger they did. For half its existence much of Washington was little more than a midden. Its site beside the Potomac, just inside the old South, was selected in 1790 when the inventors of the new nation, seeking a capital, reached a compromise between the North and the South: the South paid off war debts and in return the federal capital was planted in southern territory, in Maryland and Virginia. A French architect and engineer, Pierre L'Enfant, took out a sheet of blank paper and drew Washington's grand boulevards and Parisian circles, ideal for sauntering and ceremonials, and also ideal for rapid troop movements and mob control, with clear fields of fire, should the need arise. His plans, however, were shelved. He fell into a row over property development, and he died almost forgotten and unpaid for his master plan. It was another eighty years before men with vision and cavalier views of budgeting took hold of the plan and started building the Elysian Washington that L'Enfant had dreamed of. In the meantime the city had been an unprepossessing place, as muddy as a rugby pitch in the rain, sticky and stagnant and dopey in July, August and September, and graded by the British Foreign Office as a hardship post for diplomats.

The Irish poet, Thomas Moore, who saw the dismal and boggy capital in the early nineteenth century, wrote:

> This fam'd metropolis, where fancy sees,
> Squares in morasses, obelisks in trees;
> Which second sighted seers e'en now adorn,
> With shrines unbuilt and heroes yet unborn.

Forty years later there was not much improvement. Charles Dickens wrote of Washington as 'the headquarters of tobacco-tinctured saliva.' Americans evidently spit less now; though cheeks still bulge, chewing gum having replaced the quid. Dickens also wrote of Washington as a capital-in-waiting, calling it 'The City of Magnificent Intentions.' He added: 'It has no trade or commerce of its own: having little or no population beyond the President and his establishment: and members of the Legislature; the Government Clerks and officers, keepers of the hotels and boarding houses. It is very unhealthy. Few people would live in Washington who were not obliged to reside there.'

Although, well into the second half of the nineteenth century, pigs snuffled in Pennsylvania Avenue, Washingtonians kept alive their dream of dwelling in marble halls. They realized it in fits and starts. The construction of the George

186

Washington monument, that soaring stone stake five hundred and fifty-five feet high, fits well into the story of the city's growth. It was started in 1848 and grew to one hundred and fifty-two feet before the money ran out. It stayed there for a quarter of a century, a sad sore thumb, before work started again. Meanwhile some anti-Catholic cranks stole a marble slab, the gift of the Pope, and dumped it in the Potomac. Work resumed at last, this time with stone slightly darker, giving the effect of a suit with trousers and jacket not quite matched; but in 1884 the solid aluminium tip, fresh from display at Tiffany's, was popped on and the great digit reached for the sky, to the glory of Washington, George and city; and America. 'This shaft,' said President Hoover, who, like all presidents could see it clearly from the White House, 'is a thing of the spirit. There is about it a mantle of radiance.' Before the apex windows were glassed, five suicides wriggled out and jumped; and before the nine hundred steps were closed, silly students climbed them on their hands.

So Washington grew. Its shrines were built, its heroes were born, and died, and are commemorated; it is a truly monumental city. Greek temples, Doric columns, Corinthian columns, Roman baths, marble galleries, painted halls, florid Renaissance frescoes, heroic statuary bearing torches, swords and tomes of wisdom, scrolls and curlicues, noble porticoes, and great memorials — all white and imposing, rising from lawns and knolls, reflected in mirror-lakes, with inspirational Great Words etched upon them. It is sometimes difficult to remember that Washington in its present form is a young city, that L'Enfant's plans were only relatively recently dusted down and implemented. If its grandeur is sometimes a little selfconscious, it nevertheless has a grand style and a sweep to it. It may not have antiquity, but it is impressive; sometimes solemnly so. It is a city where a European is likely to feel at home. It is more manageable than New York: it is spacious and fairly flat, a place where breath can be drawn; and it has no skyscrapers because tall buildings are forbidden by a law which insists that the Capitol must be the tallest and its dome the dominant feature.

One of the first things that struck me about Washington, as it has struck others, is that it is a village. I rented an inexpensive

187

hotel room in the centre and was within a walk, short bus ride
or metro hop, of the Capitol, the White House, government
offices, businesses, newspaper and television offices, embas-
sies, the monuments and the treasures of the galleries and
museums, the squalid Watergate building, cinemas, the
Kennedy Center for the Performing Arts. It is one of the few
American cities — New York, Boston and San Francisco are
others — where it is possible to organize a reasonable life
around your legs and public transport. In the evenings I
walked to Georgetown to choose among its restaurants and
watch its busy pavement life. Georgetown is older than
Washington, eighteenth and early-nineteenth century red-
brick, once a port and tobacco market, and now a posh
address with its colonial character, little antique shops, bistros
and Chelsea-esque bustle. Inevitably it has its bright young
things dashing around in sports cars and spending father's
money, and giggling tipsy girls on bucks' arms; inevitably, too,
it has the kind of over-priced and over-booked restaurants
where people stand in small hopeless knots waiting for tables
to be vacated so that they may sit and be fashionable. But, to
be fair, it has some proper restaurants as well, with proper
prices and nice waitresses, and perhaps a barber shop quartet
to serenade you.

One of the small pleasures of Washington is to walk from
the hotel, put fifteen cents into a slot machine for a copy of the
Washington Post, and make for one of the numerous cafeterias for breakfast. I liked the atmosphere of Sholls, quiet,
cheap and pleasing. On each table there were prayers on a
card, one for Protestants, one for Catholics, one for Jews; a
thoughtful touch. I was lingering over coffee in one of the
cafeterias one morning when a shadow fell on my table and I
saw a black woman with black shining hair standing there
hand on hip.

'Hi, honey,' she said.

'Good morning,' I replied, uncertainly.

'I would like you to give me a baby.'

'Perhaps not just at the moment,' I said, raising my newspaper to its former height.

She gave a laugh, raised her hand to her hair and pulled it off
with a dramatic flourish. It was evident that the lady was a

188

gentleman. He laughed again and plopped the wig back, then walked off down the cafeteria. I saw that everyone around me was drinking coffee with great concentration, determined non-witnesses. I went to the cash desk and paid. As I left I saw the drama being re-enacted before the astonished gaze of another customer: the black wig was yanked with a flourish and the customer's jaw dropped like a forge-hammer.

Washington has many surprises, if not so piquant as that one. For one thing it comes as a surprise to the newcomer to find it is a city mainly of black people. Threequarters of its population is black so that blackness is a most important part of human character. Within two or three minutes' walk of the Capitol are quiet streets of brick houses where black people sit and chat on their front porches on hot afternoons, creating a southern ambience: it is as if a scene has changed suddenly on a stage. And the President has only to drive for a minute or two from the White House, beyond the lush kempt greens and equestrian statuary and smart white buildings to see the ruins of red and brown buildings sacked in race riots; and decayed streets which are a reminder of the pressing needs in this, and other, American cities.

Another surprise is the extent to which Washington is a city of chatter. It is part of the village atmosphere of Washington that most inhabitants seem to have a common interest, as if they are gathered round one parish pump. The business of Washington is government and the secondary business is government-watching. If the government is a shark the reporters are the pilot fish. Washington is the most important of the world's news centres and it is washed by waves of gossip as politicians keep an eye on each other and the journalists keep an eye on the politicians and also an eye on each other. As a focal point of world attention, of government and of lobbying, it has the largest centre in the world where the craft of serious journalism is practised. Newspaper men and television men, reporters, legmen, columnists, pundits, interpreters, commentators and gossip-seekers — they all spend their days close to politicians, civil servants, aides, lobbyists and faction spokesmen; trying to establish the real meanings of words and actions. It is a close and somewhat incestuous world, and although my experience of it was brief I found that to be

189

part of its have-you-heard? atmosphere was stimulating and absorbing.

A news editor who took me to lunch at a busy restaurant said: 'I come here about twice a week. Same table, here in the corner, so that I can see *them,* the politicians, to see who's eating with who; and people come and talk to me. I keep up-to-date.'

For a couple of weeks I worked, or rather stayed around as an observer, in the Washington bureau of *Newsweek,* courtesy of Mel Elfin, the genial, shrewd and enthusiastic bureau chief. 'I love this city,' he said. 'It must be the most exciting place in the world to work in. It is a city of world importance, a stage for great dramas, endlessly fascinating. It is not only a place of history. When I move around it I can feel that history, and feel the excitement of history in the making. The White House, the Washington monument, the Potomac, the national airport, they're all right there outside my office window. I remember the Vietnam marches, the race riots, the smoke over Washington, machine-guns on the steps of the Capitol, the curfews. This city is at the heart of the American drama: what more could a journalist want?'

The reporters I met in Washington were usually serious people writing about serious events. I envied them their position in the system of open govenment in which they worked. Information about what is done or planned in the public name is much easier to gather than it is in Britain where journalists work with a winkle-pin as well as a pen because most authorities, the government, civil service, corporations, local government and the police have a tradition of secretiveness that is only slowly being cracked. American journalists still complain of closed doors in Washington — 'Jesus, they're still holding out on us,' they would breathe as they left press conferences — but journalists live by disclosure and are always hungry for more.

The Watergate scandal was, of course, a triumph of journalism and its effects are felt still. Donald Dwight, publisher of the *Minneapolis Tribune,* said: 'It did wonders for recruiting. There was a time when newspaper reporting had a rather seedy image, but with Watergate and Nixon's downfall the image of journalism shot up in public estimation. Newspaper editors

190

found themselves dealing with far more job applications than they could handle, and this is good news for us because we can pick from a large selection. Watergate inevitably led to an over-reaction, a belief that there was a scandal behind every door in every government office, city hall and police department, just waiting for a bright young reporter to walk in and write about it; but there is a lot more to newspaper reporting than that, and people can't expect to meet Deep Throat every working day.'

In an atmosphere where reporters are on the alert for the faintest speck of dirt on politicians' hands and ferret in cupboards for skeletons, some are scrupulous about keeping their own hands clean, and take care not to get themselves compromised. I was once taken by a Washington reporter to a luncheon given by a right-wing lobbyist who wanted to put over his ferociously colonialist views on the Panama Canal treaties to a dozen or so journalists. As is proper on such occasions, I consumed a sustaining lunch and listened carefully to the rhetoric: I thought it anachronistic, an echo of a strident and arrogant America; but it taught me something of the emotions and attitudes that can be stirred by such issues.

The host said to his secretary: 'We gave them the seven dollars fifty lunch, didn't we?' She nodded, and the reporter wrote out a cheque for that amount and left without a stain on his character.

There are dozens of such occasions almost every day. Washington is made up of numerous pools of debate and discussion, and it is easy to dip into them, wallow a little, then move on to the next one. In the Senate the stenographer, his machine on a little tray slung around his neck, moved discreetly like a cigarette seller to stand next to debating senators.

In the little metro that runs from the Capitol to the Senate offices, like a fairground ghost train, men sat deep in talk; at the White House (white, I was reminded kindly, because it had to be painted after the British charred it in 1814) there was a news conference about President Carter's Middle East policy. The Health Secretary, just down the road, gave a press briefing about his ideas on smoking. I sat with some Indians who were giving evidence to a House committee. At the Pentagon, where big recessed security locks on doors are marked: Do Not Use

As Ash Tray, I listened to questions about radiation damage to servicemen ('Did you say two hundred thousand?' 'Well, somewhere in that ball park.') I dived into a hotel, showed a pass to security men and listened to General Dayan's press conference. I went to a discussion at Common Cause, one of the pressure groups — 'We started out in 1970 when citizens got together because they felt their views weren't being listened to, that Congress wasn't dealing with serious problems. We're activists. We release citizen energy. We sue people and institutions and get things done. We get allies in Congress. The general feeling in this town, and elsewhere, is that Carter's administration is incompetent. Lobbying? It's a growth industry.' I went to Ralph Nader's offices: Mr Nader, spare, ascetic, still living in the same tiny flat he has always lived in, knit his black brows in concentration — 'Of course Naderism isn't dead. It isn't a one-man show anyway. Who wants to be the Lone Ranger? The movement is consumerism and it is big and growing, and it's also becoming more specialized. We're fighting to change the system. As long as the people are being defrauded you'll have consumerism, and Congress is anti-consumer. The big corporations are the consumers' greatest enemies because they control govenment.'

Over at the splendid headquarters of the merged super-unions, AFL-CIO, George Meany, the president, was holding court at the head of a table large enough to launch planes. He was eighty-five years old when I saw him, bulldog-square, sharp-witted, gruff, monarch since 1955 of the unions he united. 'Well no, we're not very happy with Jimmy Carter's administration. We supported him strongly, but when he was elected he became a different man. He is the first small businessman elected president, and the trouble is he thinks small. Sure, there's discrimination against blacks in the unions: some unions have barred them, others have taken them in, only to meet employer resistance. We fight for equality, but you don't change the habits of a century overnight. No, we don't want the Japanese taking our jobs. No, we don't want workers sitting on company boards. What we want is our share of the wealth, and if we don't get it we go on strike. We've achieve a lot for working Americans. We never get enough, but we get plenty.'

192

In an office near Capitol hill, the people in the Center for Defense Information are the watchdogs of American military spending. 'Our job is to criticize the defence departments and come up with other options. We have an adversary relationship with the Pentagon, which is conservative and doesn't like criticism. It sure doesn't put out the welcome mat. Though most of our material comes from the Pentagon, so there are some people who appreciate what we're doing.'

Over a drink with a newspaper editor I passed on a criticism I had heard, that the press was unfair to the president. 'It's not our business to be fair. Our business is to tell.' At lunch a veteran observer said that the president presented the press with a difficulty. It was not sure what to make of him. 'He campaigned as the decent man who would restore honesty, moral values and prosperity to an America which hungered for these things, having been run by Nixon's administration of felons. But the programme had no coherence, no philosophical, ideological or sociological underpinning. And he doesn't speak much to the people. He says little that is memorable or inspiring. He hasn't managed to involve us in his hopes and dreams. He isn't an educator. He's tinkering with the car when he should be driving it. And he doesn't know the road.'

A reporter said: 'The trouble is, we want our president to be successful in everything he does. The president isn't exciting and he's no great originator, but the job is an almost impossible one. And don't forget that we voted him in.'

As the days unfolded I listened to the capital gossiping, scrapping, arguing, cajoling, whining, orating. 'Okay, you guys,' someone said at a meeting, 'let's prioritize!'

I decided to prioritize and went for a walk to blow the excess words out of my skull. I walked from the Capitol to the Washington monument, past the reflecting lake to pay respects to Lincoln, crossed the Potomac over which the jets seemed to be hauled slowly up as if by ropes, to Arlington cemetery where the wind flickered the eternal flame at the Kennedy grave, and kids stared absently at the dry carnations on the simple black stone and blew their bubble gum. Back in the city a television reporter was reciting his story to a camera. I bought a paper. After all I had been out of touch for a few hours. I thought I might try to eat the special St Valentine's Day lunch at the Pentagon the following day and go to the museum where George Washington's false teeth are kept. He looks so stern and tight-lipped in his portraits, I thought it would be pleasant to see his smile.

20
TRAILS

I have fallen in love with American names,
The sharp names that never get fat,
The snakeskin-titles of mining claims,
The plumed war-bonnet of Medicine Hat,
Tucson and Deadwood and Lost Mule Flat.
                    Stephen Vincent Benet

I fell in love with American names, too. When I was a boy I used to gaze at an atlas and read the names on the signposts of the American adventure. They evoked excitement, romance and wistfulness. They spoke of gold and gunfire, dust and blood, hard work and worn-out ploughs, deep faith and broken hopes and dreams fulfilled.

They sprang out of the pages of books and comics and were drawled and shouted on the radio and on the screen at my local Regal: Dodge, Denver and Deadwood, Abilene and Kansas City, Silver City and Cavalry Creek. I knew their hitching-rails well.

And names like Cripple Creek and Coffeyville, Broken Bow and Bloody Basin, Horse Thief Canyon, Old Dime Box and Wagon Mound, were scented with sweat and mischief. The towns of Difficult, Truth or Consequence, Hungry Horse and Gold Run also evoked the frontier. And Sweetwater and Good Thunder and Grass Valley were redolent of the plough and the beginnings of trade and the growth of order in a new-found land. Custer and Cody were named after genuine figures of the swiftly vanishing frontier. In 1942, with the old Wild West long gone, the town of Berwyn, Oklahoma, changed its name to Gene Autry, in honour of a celluloid hero.

Meanwhile, words like Kalamazoo, Chattanooga, San Francisco, Saginaw, Wichita, Memphis and Mobile, were always on the air and off the tongue; and I have a considerable repertoire of snatches of songs woven around American names which are fashioned from Indian tongues, and bits of English, Spanish and French, and which seem invented for melodies.

In my pursuit of American names it was inevitable that I should find that travelling was sometimes better than arriving. Nashville, for example, was disappointing. In the capital of country music the Grand Ole Opry was drab and shuttered. The city, like so many in America, seemed empty and lifeless in its heart when the working day was done. There was a little lack-lustre music in two or three tawdry bars; but otherwise a derelict air. For a European it takes time to adjust to the back-to-front nature of many American towns. You have to travel away from the hub and out along the spokes to find restaurants and entertainment and attractive housing. Country music now has its main shop window, not in the old downtown temple, but in a glittering new Opry House out of town. Its vast stage contains some planking from the Ole Opry, splinters off the old block.

Country music, I was surprised to learn, is only Nashville's third largest industry. The largest is Bible-punching, the printing and publishing of religious books. But it is the music that Nashville is famed for, and, in middle America especially, country music is inescapable. Like police car sirens wailing and echoing down city canyons in the small hours, it is one of the quintessential sounds of America. It is simple, sentimental, twanging, repetitious, nostalgic, lyrically banal and musically narrow, astonishingly popular and the basis of a wide stratum in the culture of the people.

Its omnipresence, though, can grow irksome. When I mentioned to someone that there seemed to be nothing else available on the car radio, he said: 'Don't worry, we do have other sorts of music in America, I promise.' And he jumped into the driving seat and began to twiddle the knobs with the crouched intensity of a ham hunting a faint short wave transmission. But after some minutes he emerged, shaking his head. 'Try a few miles further north,' he suggested, 'you might have better luck.' Some Americans say that their free-for-all broadcasting systems provide freedom of choice. In practice, though, that very freedom limits choice.

If there were disappointments in some arrivals, there were also many expectations satisfied. North of Lake Superior, Hiawatha's Gitche Gumee, at the end of the Gunflint Trail, where Minnesota and Canada meet, I propelled a canoe over Lake Saganaga. The canoe whispered and cut its vanishing furrow among shadowy islets on which pines crowded like arrows in quivers. Far off there was a lazy curl of smoke and a camp fire, a steak spitting and a warm tent; and I was at one with Natty Bumppo in the Leatherstocking Tales. Next morning, on an impluse, I dived into the crystal icy lake, emerging breathless and baptized.

Soon the snow came and the lakes of Minnesota, which in summer lie like mirrors in scattered profusion, froze over. Minnesotans began their trench war with winter. Early one morning, about two o'clock, I went to join the great queue of people at the state capitol building in St Paul who were waiting to file past the bier of Hubert Humphrey. The people's sense of loss was profound: Hubert Humphrey's political life, rooted in idealism and ideas of service, was an inspiration to many Americans. The queue shuffled throughout a freezing day and a bitter night.

Some American names, of course, were brought over in the baggage of Europeans; and it is interesting to compare places with their namesakes. Oxford, Mississippi, is also a centre of higher education, the home of the University of Mississippi, known as Ole Miss; and was the Jefferson of William Faulkner's Southern novels. In his fine old house, Rowan Oak, Faulkner's sturdy old Underwood typewriter sits on a windowside desk. I was told that if touched it doesn't write, but rings a burglar alarm.

I went South and did what many Americans like to do, or dream of doing: I escaped the harshness of the northern winter. Warmth has its part in the new growth of the South, but so does air-conditioning which makes summer working bearable.

I would have felt cheated had I not enjoyed New Orleans — and, indeed, it was all that its name had promised. In the French quarter, where romantic and seedy blend, carriages rattled among buildings whose black lace iron balconies help to give this city its piquant character. The horses wore straw hats and had the dignity of dung trays slung discreetly beneath their hindquarters. There were portrait artists out in the open, sketching tourists; and, being gentlemen and businessmen, they omitted and smoothed wrinkles, giving each husband a wife ten years younger. In Bourbon Street jazz spilled out of smoky bars, and some of the leathery old musicians played as if wound up, like clockwork drummers; and others, with eyes gazing at some distant star, set their *embouchures* to the millionth playing that week of 'When The Saints Go Marching In.'

The plane to Florida, The Dunroamin' State, final anchorage for many Americans, was full of grey heads, and at the airport were ranks of wheelchairs to meet the aged and infirm. At the hotel pool, where there was a view of the Gulf of Mexico, and gently frapping palms, men with the build of blancmanges sat in straining shorts with mouths snapped like gins on cigars, while their jewelled wives stretched out beside them like bits of rhinestoned leather. Among Florida's Edenish orange groves and lush landscaping, Walt Disney built one of his candy-coloured fantasy parks where there are monorails and submarine rides, ice creams as big as footballs, and where Mickey Mouse shakes hands. I felt that it was so clean and wholesome that had I dropped a toffee paper an electronic Goofy would have appeared to kick me.

From Disney World it was a short step to a name that symbolized scientific adventure in the 1960s — Cape Canaveral, where, in the country where everything seems possible, the moon rockets are out of the comics and on the launching pads. Their size is truly awesome — and I remembered the capsules I had seen in Washington: not much larger than catbaskets, some of them; the pinheads on the mighty shoulders of Saturns.

Some trails led me to the battlefields of the Civil War, poignant names all. An American friend told me that he and a colleague had once visited a battlefield and he, who lived in the North, had instinctively drifted over to inspect the Northern lines, while his colleague, a Southerner, had automatically set off to view the Southern lines. In the Atlanta that Sherman once flattened, the executives of Coca Cola invited me to take

Coke with them in their panelled board room. Undaunted by the recent saccharin scare, they swigged with bravado from bottles of the Product, smacking their lips the while, and refusing to divulge the famous secret ingredient, no doubt because it is disappointingly ordinary, and narrowing their eyes when someone said Pepsi.

The name of Texas still stirs up a picture of a rumbustious way of life. And there is much truth in the image. Texas is still something of a frontier state and still has its barons seeking power and advantage as barons did in medieval Europe centuries ago. It is an immensely rich state and it is becoming the energy capital of the United States. Financiers and lawyers, and all manner of opportunists, have been tumbling off the planes and running through airports to catch dollars. Houston is a boom-town which for some time has been growing at the rate of two thousand families a week. It is bustling and sprawling and throbbing with energy. It is a hive. In some quarters it has a raw edge and (as they can be in other parts of the United States) the police can be very rough. There is a strong conservative strain in Texans, a suspicion of governmental power and strong feelings against any concentrations of power, whether in oil, gas or money. There is a deep belief in Texas as a land of opportunity. The people pile in to work and to profit, and labour organization is weak.

One morning in Houston I saw a surgeon delve for a businessman's heart. Its glistening vermilion brilliance and powerful pulsating motion were awesome. Held in the surgeon's hands it was assertive and defiant, as if urgently anxious to get its owner back to work. But an artery was clogged and it was being repaired with a vein being taken from a leg. The operation cost thousands of dollars — the fees met by insurance — and the doctors would be doing several that day. Doctors, and the money they make, are the subject of considerable debate in the United States. Many Americans believe that doctors are greedy, virtually swearing the Hippocratic oath in their bank managers' offices. Big money is one of the reasons why American physicians look on British doctors as the poor victims of the socialized medicine so many of them view with horror. In the 1940s President Truman wanted to bring in national health insurance, but the doctors' lobby blocked it for twenty years, until Medicare, health insurance for the elderly, and Medicaid, insurance for the poor, were introduced. Many doctors, and many patients, too, take the view that in a free society a man should take responsibility for his family's health care, not the society in which he lives. In reality, the American way means that because of the rich pickings there are too many surgeons, too many unnecessary operations, too many people falling through the insurance net and being ruined. Because American medicine lacks a certain element of broader, humanitarian concern, many Americans live in fear and at risk.

The relationship between cash and medicine is close; America is a country where you can sell your blood, which seems bizarre and faintly offensive to me, and where, because there is a web of commercial and public ambulance services, you might be charged to be scooped off the street. Once, taken to hospital myself, I was put in a waiting-room; but it was not a waiting-room for a doctor, but for an accountant. Only when the accountant was satisfied about the manner in which I would pay for treatment was I sent to a doctor's waiting-room.

A friend of mine, a foreigner in the United States, was treated by a doctor for a minor ailment. 'I know American doctors have a bad name abroad for going after every cent they can get,' the doctor said. 'There'll be no charge. We're not all like that.'

I do not suppose that any American name has stimulated more visions and dreams and shivers of excitement than California. The Spaniards named it after the fabulous Shangri-La island described in a popular tale of chivalry and quest written in the fifteenth century; and a dream land it has always been and a dream land it remains for many. Especially the millions who have a high standard of living. It is lush, sunny and gorgeous. It has vineyards and tens of thousands of long-legged tawny-skinned girls with excellent teeth, stamped out in a California Girls factory close to a dazzling white beach on the blue Pacific coast. There is a whole tribe of psychiatrists dedicated to unknotting the minds of the aimless and unfortunate who cannot cope with the strains of life in what seems, to many insiders as well as outsiders, a blessed and sunny land. People still come to pan for gold in their own ways; Chicanos

200

swell the *barrios* of Los Angeles, and other Americans come to live under that vast smoggy dome. The directors, entrepreneurs and hangers-on of the film industry are still drawn to Hollywood where the prizes are glittering. In a Hollywood restaurant one night a waitress really did tell me that she had travelled there from the mid-west to seek fame and money in the film industry. Already, she said, her hand had been seen in a television commercial. For the better life, for the freedom to cruise the majestic highways of this state, some Californians have already shown that they will kill to get a few gallons of the petrol that fuels the better life. In San Francisco, against all the odds, the clanking street cars beetle up steep hills. They are eccentric and perhaps inefficient; but they are a lovable motif of that most refreshing of cities and their serpentine antics are a proper defiance of the increasing homogeneity of much of the United States.

During my travels, and arrivals, there were times when I had views of the seemingly intractable problems of the modern American experience. I saw things lurid, distasteful, foul, bleak and wretched and cruel. But for most of the pessimistic conclusions I had drawn there was an optimistic contradiction. The depressing things I saw tempered, but did not flatten, my sense of excitement; and I look forward to renewing the affair.

Just before I left, in some clear sharp days on the edge of spring, I travelled through the Grand Teton mountains and the Yellowstone region of Wyoming. One morning, just after daybreak, I set off to explore Yellowstone, and Old Faithful geyser huffed and puffed behind me as I started. I walked for some miles. Geysers fizzed, plopped, gurgled, roared and spat, and steam clouds drifted over grazing elk, moose and bison. There was a pungent and sulphurous smell, as if witches were brewing among the trees. There was no one about and there was, withal, an air of the primeval. It was eerie and enchanting. I felt, as I had felt before on occasions, the excitement of America, something of its primitiveness and rawness, its age, vastness and grandeur.

INDEX